The
Abingdon Worship
Annual 2015

Edited by
Mary J. Scifres
and B.J. Beu

Abingdon Press / Nashville

The Abingdon Worship Annual 2015

Copyright © 2014 by Abingdon Press

This book is printed on acid-free paper.

ISBN 978-1-4267-7967-1

14 15 16 17 18 19 20 21 22 23—10 9 8 7 6 5 4 3 2 1

MANUFACTURED IN THE UNITED STATES OF AMERICA

Contents

CONTENTS

CONTENTS

November 26, 2015 *Thanksgiving Day* 262
November 29, 2015 *First Sunday of Advent* 267

December
December 6, 2015 *Second Sunday of Advent* 272
December 13, 2015 *Third Sunday of Advent* 277
December 20, 2015 *Fourth Sunday of Advent* 282
December 24, 2015 *Christmas Eve* 290
December 27, 2015 *First Sunday after Christmas* 295

Contributors 301

Indexes
Scripture Index 305
Communion Liturgy Index 310

Online Contents
The following materials are found only in the Abingdon Worship Annual 2015 section at www.abingdonpress.com/downloads. Instructions on how to view these materials in your browser or download them to your computer are available at the site. PLEASE NOTE: This file is password protected (see page 312 below).
Full Text of the Print Edition i-312
Introduction to Additional Resources 314
2015 Lectionary Calendar 316
Hymn and Song Suggestions 317
Web Worship Resource Suggestions 328
Lectionary Setting for November 1, 2015 336
Worship Resources for Communion 341
    Invitations 341
    Great Thanksgivings 343
    Prayers and Responses 360

vi

Introduction

The worship landscape has changed so much over the past twenty years that worship leaders are feeling overwhelmed. In the "good old days," if worship planners coordinated Scripture with liturgy, preaching, and hymns, they were good to go. And if the choir anthem actually fit the theme, worship was considered amazing. Now, worship leaders are faced with demands for diverse music and worship styles, and eye-catching on-screen presentations. Add in multimedia, visuals, texting, tweeting, and visitors "liking" your church on Facebook (during worship), and the pressures placed upon worship planners can become overwhelming.

That is where this resource comes in. In *The Abingdon Worship Annual 2015*, we provide theme ideas and all the written and spoken elements of worship, following the *Revised Common Lectionary*. (Although this resource does not address the visual and emerging resources that many worship services require, Mary Scifres Ministries has added an online resource to do just that at: http://maryscifres.com/Worship_Subscription.html.) *The Abingdon Worship Annual 2015* offers words for worship that provide the framework for congregations to participate fully in the liturgical life of worship.

For basic song and hymn suggestions, as well as on-line access to the hard copy materials, we include Internet access for each worship service at abingdonpress.com/downloads. See page 312 for instructions on accessing the download. The web link allows you to import printed prayers and responsive readings directly into your bulletins for ease of use and printing. In addition to the hymn and song suggestions, the online link includes some bonus material: worship resources for lectionary alternatives not included in the hard copy, worship website suggestions, and an extensive compilation of communion resources.

In *The Abingdon Worship Annual 2015*, you will find the words of many different authors, poets, pastors, laypersons, and theologians. Some authors have written for this resource before, others provide a fresh voice. Since the contributing authors represent a wide variety of denominational and theological backgrounds, their words will vary in style and content. Feel free to combine or adjust the words within these pages to fit the needs of your congregation and the style of your worship. (Notice the reprint permission for worship given on the copyright page of this book.)

Each entry provides suggestions that follow an order of service that may be adapted to address your specific worship practice and format. Feel free to reorder or pick and choose the various resources to fit the needs of your worship services and congregations. Each entry follows a thematic focus arising from one or more of the week's scriptures.

To fit the Basic Pattern of Christian Worship—reflecting a flow that leads from a time of gathering and praise, into a time of receiving and responding to the Word, and ending with a time of sending forth—each entry includes Contemporary Gathering Words, Call to Worship and Opening Prayer, Prayer of Confession and Words of Assurance, Response to the Word, Offertory Prayer, and Benedictions.

Communion Resources are offered in selected entries. Additional ideas are also provided throughout this resource.

Some readers find the Contemporary Gathering Words or Unison Prayers helpful as "Centering Words" that may be printed in a worship handout or projected on a screen. Use the words offered here in the way that best suits your congregation's spiritual needs, and please remember to give copyright and author credit!

Using the Worship Resources

Contemporary Gathering Words and **Calls to Worship** gather God's people together as they prepare to worship. Often called "Greetings" or "Gathering Words," these words may be read by one worship leader or be read responsively. Regardless of how they are printed in this resource, feel free to experiment in your services of worship. They may be read antiphonally (back and forth) between two readers or two groups within the congregation: women and men, choir and musicians, young people and old, and so on.

Opening Prayers in this resource are varied in form, but typically invoke God's presence into worship. Whether formal, informal, general, or specific, these prayers serve to attune our hearts and minds to God. Although many may be adapted for use in other parts of the worship service, we have grouped them into the category "Opening Prayers."

Prayers of Confession and **Words of Assurance** lead the people of God to acknowledge our failing while assuring us of God's forgiveness and grace. Regardless of how they are printed, whether unison or responsively, Prayers of Confession and Words of Assurance may be spoken by a single leader or led by a small group. Some prayers may even be used as Opening or Closing Prayers.

Litanies and **Responsive Readings** offer additional avenues of congregational participation in our services of worship. Think creatively as you decide how to use these **Responsive Readings** in your service of worship: in unison, by a worship leader alone, or in a call and response format. Feel free to change the title of these liturgies to suit your worship setting.

Benedictions, sometimes called "Blessings" or "Words of Dismissal" send the congregation forth to continue the work of worship. Some of these Benedictions work best in call and response format, others work best when delivered as a blessing by a single worship leader. As always, use the format best suited to your congregation.

In response to requests from many of our readers, we have provided a number of **Communion** liturgies as well, each written specifically to relate to the thematic and scriptural focus of the day. Some follow the pattern of the Great Thanksgiving; others are Invitations to Communion or Communion Prayers of Consecration for the celebration of the Eucharist.

Although you will find *The Abingdon Worship Annual 2015* an invaluable tool for planning worship, it is but one piece of the puzzle for worship preparation. For additional music suggestions, you will want to consult *Prepare! An Ecumenical Music and Worship Planner*, or *The United Methodist Music and Worship Planner*. These resources contain lengthy listings of lectionary-related hymns, praise songs, vocal solos, and choral anthems. For video, screen visual, and secular song along with experiential worship ideas for each Sunday, subscribe to Mary Scifres Ministries' new online resource *Worship Plans and Ideas* at http://maryscifres.com/Worship_Subscription.html.

As you begin your worship planning, read the scriptures for each day, then meditate on the **Theme Ideas** suggested in this resource. Review the many words for worship printed herein and listen for the words that speak to you. Trust God's guidance, and enjoy a wonderful year of worship and praise!

Mary J. Scifres and B. J. Beu, Editors
The Abingdon Worship Annual
beuscifres@gmail.com

Learn more about workshop and training opportunities through Mary Scifres Ministries at www.maryscifres.com.

January 4, 2015

Epiphany of the Lord

B. J. Beu

[Copyright © 2014 by B. J. Beu. Used by permission.]

Color

White

Scripture Readings

Isaiah 60:1-6; Psalm 72:1-7, 10-14; Ephesians 3:1-12;
Matthew 2:1-12

Theme Ideas

Today's scripture readings are much more than a celebration of kings bringing tribute to the Messiah—they
are a promise of light to those who live in darkness;
a promise of righteousness to those who suffer at the
hands of others; a promise of grace to those who are lost;
and a promise of salvation to the Gentiles. Epiphany is
a day to celebrate God's love for all—especially those
who are most in need of God's light and love.

Invitation and Gathering

Contemporary Gathering Words (Isaiah 60, Matthew 2)
Look around, God's light shines in the darkness.
The darkness fades like the waning night.

1

Look about you, God's glory is all around.
Our hearts sing with joy.
Look up, Christ's star has risen in the sky.
We will follow the light of the world.

Call to Worship (Isaiah 60)

Arise, shine, for your light has come.
The glory of the Lord shines like the sun.
Behold, the nations have come to witness God's light.
Kings have come to behold Christ's brightness.
Lift up your eyes and look around.
The glory of the Lord has come.

—Or—

Call to Worship (Psalm 72)

The Holy One rules.
Let those who oppress the poor tremble.
The God of heaven and earth is righteous.
Let those who stray return to the Lord.
The Eternal Judge is seated in the judgment chair.
Let those who love justice shout for joy.
The Holy One rules.
Let us worship.

Opening Prayer (Matthew 2)

Glorious God,
grant us the courage to follow Christ's natal star,
wherever your light would lead us;
grant us the wisdom to follow the kings of old,
as they left the safety of their homes
to find the infant Jesus;
grant us the purity of heart,
to forsake the glitter of things that do not endure,
and embrace the brightness of your glory.

2

Proclamation and Response

Prayer of Confession (Matthew 2)
Eternal God,
following only a star in the sky,
kings of old left their families and their lands
to find a child whose birth was so profound,
it was proclaimed in the heavens above.
When we would rather sit comfortably in our homes
than make spiritual pilgrimages of our own,
clothe our feet of clay in walking shoes
and send us on our way.
At this season of light,
help us shine your light in the darkness
to honor the King of kings.
Open our shut-up hearts to those in need,
that the gifts of gold, frankincense, and myrrh
might not be the last gifts offered to the one
who brings light into our lives. Amen.

Assurance of Pardon (Matthew 2, Ephesians 3)
The power that brought light and salvation
to the kings of old is at work in the world today,
granting eternal life to those who turn to God.

Response to the Word (Psalm 72)
Let justice roll down like waters,
and righteousness like an ever-flowing stream.
Let the voice of the needy be heard throughout the land,
and the plea of the widow be answered.
Let God be praised and Christ proclaimed,
and let the whole world see the glory of our God.

3

Thanksgiving and Communion

Offering Prayer (Psalm 72)
>Merciful God,
>>may your justice roll down like waters,
>>may your righteousness flow
>>>like an ever-flowing stream.
>May these gifts and offerings be an answer to your call—
>>a call to deliver the needy, rescue the weary,
>>>and defend the poor and the defenseless. Amen.

Sending Forth

Benediction (Isaiah 60, Psalm 72)
>Go forth as a light to the nations.
>>**We go forth, following the star of Christ's birth.**
>Go forth as a people of blessing.
>>**We go forth, proclaiming hope**
>>**to the poor and needy.**
>Go forth as a light to the nations.
>>**We go forth, with God's blessings.**

>*—Or—*

Benediction (Matthew 2)
>Follow the kings of old in search of God's Son.
>>**We go with the promise of new life in Christ.**
>Follow the Magi in search of meaning and purpose.
>>**We go with the promise of new life in Christ.**

January 11, 2015

Baptism of the Lord
Deborah Sokolove

Color

White

Scripture Readings

Genesis 1:1-5; Psalm 29; Acts 19:1-7; Mark 1:4-11

Theme Ideas

God is the creator of all things—the bringer of light and order to everything that is, a gift beyond our imaginings. God cares for us and all of creation. Just as Jesus knew himself as God's beloved child when he rose from the baptismal waters, God comes to us as the Holy Spirit in our baptism, bringing spiritual gifts and bathing us in divine love.

Invitation and Gathering

Contemporary Gathering Words (Psalm 29)
The voice of the Holy One calls to us,
pouring out love in an endless stream.
Let us worship the God who calls us.

Call to Worship (Genesis 1, Psalm 29)
>The voice of the Holy One flashes forth,
>filling the world with awe and delight.
>>**The God of light sits enthroned in holy splendor.**
>The voice of the Holy One cries out,
>bathing the world in goodness and hope.
>>**The God of glory thunders, full of majesty.**
>The voice of the Holy One calls to us from the waters,
>pouring out love in an endless stream.
>>**Let us worship the God who calls us.**

Opening Prayer (Genesis 1, Acts 19, Mark 1)
>Holy Maker of all that is and ever will be,
>>in the beginning, you breathed over primal waters:
>>>speaking light out of darkness,
>>>separating evening from morning,
>>>creating the first night and the first day.
>When Jesus rose from the waters of his baptism,
>>you spoke again, calling him your holy child
>>>as the Holy Spirit descended upon him
>>>>like a dove.
>When Paul baptized the new believers at Corinth,
>>your Holy Spirit came upon them,
>>>pouring out words of prophesy and story.
>In this day of celebration and memory,
>>fill us with your word and bathe us in your Spirit,
>>>that we may know ourselves as
>>>>beloved children,
>>>ready to give of ourselves
>>>>for the sake of the world. Amen.

Proclamation and Response

Prayer of Confession (Acts 19, Mark 1)
Holy Maker, Holy Breath, Holy Word,
you call us to turn toward your holy light.
Instead, we close our eyes
to what you would have us see,
as we are lured into dark alleyways
of selfishness and greed.
You call us to care for our neighbors as ourselves,
and to love the world that you have created.
Instead, we look for reasons to hate and mistrust,
putting our own desires
ahead of the needs of others.
You call us to put our faith in you,
and know that everyone is your beloved child.
Forgive us, Holy One,
for we have forgotten our baptismal promises,
looking to ourselves rather than to you
for our salvation.

Words of Assurance (Acts 19:1-7; Mark 1:4-11)
The Holy One pours out love and grace,
forgiving all who repent and turn away from sin.
You are God's beloved.
In you God is well pleased.
You are God's beloved.
In you God is well pleased.
Glory to God. Amen.

Passing the Peace of Christ (Mark 1:4-11)
As beloved children of God, let us share signs of peace
with one another.

The peace of Christ be with you.
The peace of Christ be with you, always.

Prayer of Preparation (Genesis 1, Psalm 29, Acts 19, Mark 1)
Holy Word, Holy Maker, Holy Breath,
you spoke and the light appeared,
beginning the orderly procession of days
and the ongoing story of creation.
Help us know the world in the light of your truth,
that we might hear your voice
in the Word that is more than words.
Amen.

Response to the Word (Genesis 1, Acts 19, Mark 1)
In our baptism, we become one with Christ,
who is a beacon of light in a dark, chaotic world.

Thanksgiving and Communion

Invitation to the Offering (Genesis 1, Psalm 29, Acts 19, Mark 1)
Rejoicing in the love which God has poured out on us,
let us bring our gifts and offerings to the Holy One.

Offering Prayer (Genesis 1, Psalm 29, Acts 19, Mark 1)
Holy Lover, Holy Beloved One,
Source and End of all love,
we return these gifts to you. Amen.

Great Thanksgiving
Christ be with you.
And also with you.
Lift up your hearts.

We lift them up to God.
Let us give our thanks to the Holy One.
It is right to give our thanks and praise.

It is a right, good, and a joyful thing,
always and everywhere to give our thanks to you,
creator of days and nights, trees and mountains,
water and fire, and all that lives and breathes.
We give thanks that you have given us this lovely world,
filled with fish and flowers, cattle and birds,
bright, blue mornings, and velvet nights
filled with stars, roaring seas, and
gently rolling rivers.
We give thanks for all our days and nights,
for morning and evening and all the love
you pour out on us and on all that you have made.
And so, with your creatures on earth
and all the heavenly chorus,
we praise your name and join their unending hymn:
Holy, holy, holy Lord, God of power and might,
heaven and earth are full of your glory.
Hosanna in the highest. Blessed is the one
who comes in the name of the Lord.
Hosanna in the highest.
Holy are you, and holy is your child, Jesus Christ,
who came up from the waters of baptism
to see the heavens open,
your loving voice floating like a dove
above his head.
On the night in which he gave himself up,
Jesus took bread, gave thanks to you,
broke the bread, and gave it to the disciples, saying:

"Take, eat; this is my body which is given for you.
Do this in remembrance of me."
When the supper was over, Jesus took the cup,
offered thanks and gave it to the disciples, saying:
"Drink from this, all of you;
this is my life in the new covenant,
poured out for you and for many,
for the forgiveness of sins.
Do this, as often as you drink it,
in remembrance of me."
And so, in remembrance of your mighty acts
in Jesus Christ, we proclaim the mystery of faith.
Christ has died.
Christ is risen.
Christ will come again.
Pour out your Holy Spirit on us,
and on these gifts of bread and wine.
Make them be for us the body and blood of Christ,
that we may be the body of Christ
to a world drowning in chaos and pain.

Holy Lover, Beloved, Source and End of all love,
we praise your holy, eternal, loving name. Amen.

Sending Forth

Benediction (Acts 19, Mark 1)
Go into the world as the light of Christ,
pouring out love like a living stream.
May the God who is love
bless you and make you a blessing
to a world yearning to know how to love. Amen.

January 18, 2015

Second Sunday after the Epiphany

B. J. Beu

Color

Green

Scripture Readings

1 Samuel 3:1-10 (11-20); Psalm 139:1-6, 13-18;
1 Corinthians 6:12-20; John 1:43-51

Theme Ideas

God's call and our spiritual journey are never disem-
bodied affairs. God calls Samuel three times while he
is lying down and then promises to utter words that
will make our ears tingle. The psalmist marvels at being fearfully and wonderfully made. Paul warns us that
our bodies are temples of the Holy Spirit and we should
therefore glorify God in how we treat our bodies. Finally, Nathaniel is convinced to follow Jesus because Jesus
"saw" him sitting under a fig tree. Whether we are lying
down or merely growing in our mother's wombs, God
searches us and knows us, comes to us and ministers
to us, and is with us and within us. With such indwell-

ing of body and Spirit, how can we fail to respond to God's call like Samuel: "Speak, Lord, for your servant is listening."

Invitation and Gathering

Contemporary Gathering Words (Psalm 139)
Let all who draw breath praise the living God.
Let all who know the Lord sing and shout for joy.
Let all who love the Lord come and worship.

Call to Worship (1 Samuel 3, Psalm 139, John 1)
The One who knit us together in our mother's womb
is calling us today.
Speak to us, Lord, for your servants are listening.
The One who knows our paths,
the One acquainted with all our ways,
is here to lead us into life.
Lead us, O God, for we will follow.
The One who hems us in, from behind and before,
is with us in our time of worship.
Bless us, Holy One.
Put your words in our mouths
and your joy in our hearts.
Speak to us, Lord, for your servants are listening.

Opening Prayer (1 Samuel 3, Psalm 139, John 1)
Wisdom of the ages,
you know all things in heaven and on earth.
Before we were formed in our mother's womb,
you set the length of our days.
Even before a word is on our lips,
you know it completely.

You hem us in, before and behind,
    and lay your hand upon us.
Such knowledge is too wonderful for us,
    it is so high we cannot attain it.
Even in our humanness, you love us.
Even in our weakness, you call and lead us.
Call us once more, O God.
Call us, that we might hear your voice
    and respond with expectation and joy:
        "Here I am." Amen.

Proclamation and Response

Prayer of Confession (1 Samuel 3, Psalm 139, John 1)
God of a thousand voices,
    you call us when we lie down to sleep;
    you call us when we sit under a tree;
    you call us when your Spirit resides within us;
    you call us when we gather
        with family and friends.
How many times, like Samuel before us,
    have we mistaken your call
        or dismissed it as a dream?
How many times have we heard your call,
    yet remained in our beds,
        too comfortable and set in our ways
            to be bothered to respond at all?
How many times have we passed up the chance
    to listen to your messengers
        because of who they are
            or where they came from?
Forgive us, Holy One.

Speak to us once more,
>and set our ears to tingling,
>>that we may know the power of your words
>>and the glory of your ways,
>>>through Christ, our Lord. Amen.

Words of Assurance (1 Corinthians 6, John 1)
The one who says, "Follow me" never gives up on us
>and never forsakes us.
United with Christ, we are one spirit with God.
United with Christ, we are forgiven and made whole.

Passing the Peace of Christ (John 1)
The one who searches us and knows us is the one who hems us in with holy love and brings us peace. In gratitude and thanksgiving, let us turn to one another and share signs of the peace of Christ.

Introduction to the Word (1 Samuel 3)
Listen, the voice of God is calling.
Speak, Lord, for your servant is listening.

Response to the Word (1 Samuel 3, Psalm 139, 1 Corinthians 6, John 1)
The call of God touches our minds
>with knowledge and purpose.
The call of God touches our hearts
>with love and joy.
The call of God touches our bodies
>with Spirit and truth.
The call of God touches every fiber of our being
>and seeks our response:
>**"Here I am, for you called me."**

Thanksgiving and Communion

Invitation to the Offering (John 1)

Can anything good come out of a backwater town called Nazareth? Come and see. Can this church really be the living, breathing body of Christ? Come and see. Can this fellowship and the gifts we bring really make a difference in the world? Come and see. Please give generously this morning, as we invite a hurting world to "come and see."

Offering Prayer (1 Samuel 3, Psalm 139, 1 Corinthians 6, John 1)

God of vision and courage, God of solace and hope,
>you search us and know us;
>you are acquainted with all our ways.

We praise you for making our bodies
>the temple of your Spirit.

We thank you for calling us, even in the dead of night,
>to hear your voice and answer your call.

In a world so full of need,
>use our gifts and our offerings,
>>our time and our talents,
>>>to transform possibilities into realities.

Through these gifts,
>may others come and see your grace,
>>that they may hear your call in their lives. Amen.

Sending Forth

Benediction (1 Samuel 3, 1 Corinthians 6, John 1)

Go forth and speak words of love—
words that cause ears to tingle and eyes to sparkle.

**We go to speak words of hope and faith—
words that cause hearts to leap
and spirits to dance with joy.**
Go forth as the body of Christ, inviting others
to undertake their own journeys of faith.
**We go forth to remind the world
that God is speaking still.**

January 25, 2015

Third Sunday after the Epiphany
Mary J. Scifres

[Copyright © 2014 by Mary J. Scifres. Used by permission.]

Color

Green

Scripture Readings

Jonah 3:1-5, 10; Psalm 62:5-12; 1 Corinthians 7:29-31; Mark 1:14-20

Theme Ideas

Today's scriptures call us to answer God's call and share the grace we have received. In so doing, we find that God is the great equalizer and a refuge for all. Neither sin nor perfection, poverty nor riches, mourning nor rejoicing, can separate us from the love of God. Even the infamous Ninevites find forgiveness when they repent of their sins and turn once again to God. Likewise, the psalmist finds refuge in God and reminds us that earthly riches are not the power that comforts. God's love is the gift that equalizes the powerful and powerless alike, when we rest in God's refuge. Paul reminds us that all will be equal in the time that is coming. Living this equality now brings its own power and refuge. Even Jesus' calling of the first disciples is a vivid reminder that God's realm comes to us through fishermen and tax collectors, not just through religious and political leaders. God's grace is the great leveler, it makes us all one.

Invitation and Gathering

Contemporary Gathering Words (Psalm 62)
Wait in silence. Rest assured that God is present here.
Open your heart. Find the God that dwells within.
Hope in God, and trust this truth:
    God's love and grace are yours.
Optional response between each phrase if used as a responsive Call to Worship or Call to Prayer:
    God is present here.

Call to Worship (Mark 1, Jonah 3, Psalm 62)
Christ calls:
Drop your nets and come to God.
    We will follow with love.
Christ calls:
Lay your worries down and rest in the Lord.
    We will follow with hope.
Christ calls:
Release your sorrows and the burden of your guilt.
    We will follow with faith.
The God of grace, the Christ of love,
welcomes and calls us here.

Opening Prayer (Psalm 62)
God of love and grace,
    as you welcome us here this day,

we also welcome you
   to be within and among us.
Breathe your love and grace
   into our very being,
      that we may look upon one another
         with the same equanimity
            that you show to all creation.
Open our hearts,
      that we may know the truth of your presence
      and the glory of your love.

Proclamation and Response

Prayer of Confession (Jonah 3, Mark 1)
Forgive us, O God,
      for the harm we have caused others,
      for the times we have turned away from you,
      for the ways we have rejected your love and mercy.
Forty minutes, forty days, or even forty years
      would not be sufficient
         to make up for all the sins
            and errors of humankind.
But your grace is sufficient for us.
Your presence is all we need,
      each and every moment of our lives.
Forgive us, O God,
      and invite us to begin again.
Call us to follow you,
      and we will leave our nets behind.
Invite us to begin again,
      and we will accept your loving offer,
         and become a new creation,

        called and reclaimed
           in the Spirit of your love.

Words of Assurance (Mark 1)

The kingdom of God has come near.
God's realm is in our very midst.
Believe in this good news:
    In the name of Jesus Christ,
    we are forgiven and reclaimed by God.

Passing the Peace of Christ (Jonah 3, Mark 1)

Like the people of Ninevah, we have received the grace
of God's forgiveness. Let us rejoice in the gift of new beginnings as we share signs of peace and joy as followers
of Christ.

Introduction to the Word (Jonah 3, Mark 1)

God speaks in many ways.
Christ calls to one and all.
Listen, for God is still speaking,
    and Christ is still calling.

Response to the Word (Jonah 3, 1 Corinthians 7, Mark 1)

The Ninevites were held back by their sin.
The disciples were weighed down by their nets.
The Corinthians were burdened by their possessions
    and their status.
Let us lay down all those things
    that prevent us from following God,
    for Christ is calling now.
*(Participants may be invited to write a burden on a piece of
paper, bring it forward, and "lay it down" in an offering plate,
or to simply pray their burden into a symbolic object.)*

Prayer of Response (Mark 1)
>Our nets are heavy, O God,
>>with the burdens and worries of our lives.
>Take them from us,
>>that we may leave our nets behind
>>>and follow you in freedom and joy.

Thanksgiving and Communion

Invitation to the Offering (Mark 1)
>Having left our nets behind, we are called by Christ to new waters of hope. Let us answer this call as we share our gifts freely with love and joy.

Offering Prayer (1 Corinthians 7, Mark 1)
>Bless these gifts, O God,
>>that those who most need to know your love,
>>>may receive it through these gifts
>>>>and the ministries they support. Amen.

Sending Forth

Benediction (Mark 1)
>Follow Christ into the world,
>>leaving your nets and burdens here.
>Go with God into the world,
>>offering love to those you meet.

February 1, 2015

<u>Fourth Sunday after the Epiphany</u>
Joanne Carlson Brown

Color

Green

Scripture Readings

Deuteronomy 18:15-20; Psalm 111; 1 Corinthians 8:1-13; Mark 1:21-28

Theme Ideas

Knowledge. Authority. Who has them? From whom do they come? These are familiar questions, not only in biblical times, but in the twenty-first century as well. Who should we listen to? How will we know who is speaking the truth and acting from good intentions? Scripture's answer is clear: Knowledge and authority come from the one true God, and the mark and manner of that God is love. When people act in love, considering others before themselves, and keep God's covenant, they are worth listening to and following, for they will lead us in the way of God and the footsteps of Jesus.

Invitation and Gathering

Contemporary Gathering Words (Deuteronomy 18, 1 Corinthians 8, Mark 1)

What have you come expecting?

We want someone to tell us what to do and think.

Is that what you really want?

We seek knowledge and direction
from one who speaks and acts with authority.

You seek Jesus. Will you listen to him
and follow where he leads?

Yes, if God will help us.

Come then, let us open our hearts to follow the one
who speaks and acts with authority.

Call to Worship (Psalm 111, 1 Corinthians 8)

Come, those seeking wisdom and truth.

We come giving thanks to God
with our whole heart.

Come, commit yourselves again in covenant
with our God.

We come in faithfulness to receive and to live
the ways of the Holy One.

Come, let us worship in wisdom and truth,
praising our God, always and forever.

Opening Prayer (Deuteronomy 18, Psalm 111, 1 Corinthians 8, Mark 1)

God of our lives, we come this morning
seeking your wisdom and guidance.

How may we truly be your people?

How do we discern the true from the false prophets
in our midst?

How do we avoid causing another to stumble
    while giving others the courage to change?
How do we live faithfully in covenant with you?
Fill us with your wisdom, Spirit,
    and enliven us with your word,
        that we may be renewed as the people
            you have called us to be. Amen.

Proclamation and Response

Prayer of Confession (Deuteronomy 18, Psalm 111, 1 Corinthians 8, Mark 1)

God of all understanding and wisdom,
    we need your help to guide us.
Sometimes we lose our way,
    listening to the myriad voices
        that claim to speak your word and truth.
Sometimes we confuse our ways with your ways,
    causing our sisters and brothers to stumble.
Give us hands to reach out in service,
    not to reach out and grasp what we can get.
Give us the courage to change our ways.
Give us a heart to discern your truth and your voice.
Give us ears to hear, eyes to see,
    and minds to understand your ways.
Give us lips to praise you forever.
Forgive us when we lose our way—
    your way—
        and lead us back to the path
            that leads to you. Amen.

Words of Assurance (Psalm 111)

God has sent redemption to God's people.
Rejoice and be glad, for faithfulness to God

is the beginning of wisdom,
and all who practice it have a good understanding.
Claim this knowledge and be a covenant people,
beloved and cherished
in the eyes and heart of God.

Passing the Peace of Christ (Psalm 111, 1 Corinthians 8)

Greet those around you with these words:
"May you be a person of wisdom and
understanding."
Respond with the words:
"I will be, with God's help."

Introduction to the Word (Mark 1)

Listen carefully and you will hear of one who speaks
and acts with authority—one who can lead you to wisdom and understanding and faithfulness to God.

Response to the Word (Psalm 111, Mark 1)

For the wisdom we have heard;
for the call that has touched our hearts;
for the authority that comes from above,
we praise and thank God with our whole heart.

Thanksgiving and Communion

Invitation to the Offering (Psalm 111, 1 Corinthians 8)

We have been called to reach out in understanding, in
service, and in love. Our morning offering will enable
this church community to be a beacon of hope and
wisdom and service to those in the community who
so desperately need to hear and see it enacted in their
midst.

Offering Prayer (Psalm 111, 1 Corinthians 8, Mark 1)
Transform this offering into actions of love,
understanding, healing, and service.
Transform our very lives,
that we may be obedient and faithful servants
to your people in a hurting world. Amen.

Sending Forth

Benediction (Psalm 111, 1 Corinthians 8, Mark 1)
Go forth into God's world
in faithful covenant with our God.
Go forth into God's world
to be instruments of Jesus' healing touch.
Go forth into God's world
to live out the Spirit's gift
of wisdom and understanding. Amen.

February 8, 2015

Fifth Sunday after the Epiphany
Mary J. Scifres

Color

Green

Scripture Readings

Isaiah 40:21-31; Psalm 147:1-11, 20c; 1 Corinthians 9:16-23; Mark 1:29-39

Theme Ideas

While God's power is a prominent theme in all of today's scriptures, the Hebrew scripture lessons emphasize God's power for the powerless, the weak, and the broken. Those who wait and hope for God will be lifted up, healed, and strengthened. The healing of Simon's mother-in-law exemplifies the way Jesus embodies God's strength and healing power for those who wait and hope. In this passage, "making disciples" is not achieved by preaching and healing, but simply by bringing people directly to Jesus for healing and strength. All who are in need are invited to wait and hope, for God's power heals and strengthens the weak.

Invitation and Gathering

Contemporary Gathering Words (Isaiah 40)
Wait for the Lord...
even when waiting isn't easy or comfortable.
Wait, hope, wait.
Wait with hope and trust...
even when God's presence isn't obvious or clear.
Wait, hope, wait.
Wait for Christ to heal you...
even when sickness and sorrow overwhelm you.
Wait, hope, wait.
As we worship our God this day,
know that the Spirit is with us now.

Call to Worship (Isaiah 40)
Call on the name of God,
for God has called us by name.
Lift your eyes and see,
for Christ is in this place.
Know that God is near,
for the Spirit lives in each of us gathered here.

Opening Prayer (Isaiah 40)
Holy One, Creator God,
renew our strength this day.
Lift us up on your wings of love,
and guide us with your ancient wisdom and truth.
Empower us to be your people,
that all may know the power of your love.

Proclamation and Response

Call to Confession (Isaiah 40)
Come, all who are tired and weary. God's strength renews our lives.

Prayer of Confession or Prayer for Healing (Isaiah 40, Mark 1)
Holy One, you know the burdens of our hearts,
the exhaustions of our lives,
the illnesses that threaten to destroy us.
Lift our burdens.
Renew our strength.
Heal our ills, in body and soul.
(A time of silence may follow.)

Words of Assurance (Isaiah 40)
Don't you know? Haven't you heard?
God's love is more powerful than death.
God's strength is unending and true.
In God's powerful strength and love,
you are renewed and restored to life.

Introduction to the Word (Isaiah 40)
Have you not known? Have you not heard? The everlasting God, who created this earth, speaks to those who listen and wait. Listen, wait, hope...for God is speaking to us now.

Response to the Word (Isaiah 40)
Do you not know? Have you not heard?
God is everlasting and true,
powerful and mighty in love.
Do you not know? Have you not heard?

God doesn't grow tired and weary.
Do you not know? Have you not heard?
God gives power to the faint,
and strength to the powerless.
Wait in hope and trust.
We wait. We hope. We trust.
(A time of silence may follow to reflect on one's burdens. Alternately, invite people to place on the altar an object, provided earlier, that symbolizes the burdens that exhaust and overwhelm us.)
Hear these words of promise:
God will renew your strength.
We will fly upon wings like eagles.
We will run the race and not become tired.
We will follow Christ and not grow weary,
We will tell the world what we have heard,
and what we know to be true:
God is everlasting and true,
powerful and mighty in love.

Thanksgiving and Communion

Invitation to the Offering (Isaiah 40, Mark 1)
As we offer our gifts to God, we acknowledge our awareness that the world is full of sickness and sorrow, and in need of healing and hope. Bring your gifts, trusting that God will transform them into power and strength for the world.

Offering Prayer (Isaiah 40)
Bless these gifts
with your creative strength and power, O God,
that those who need to know your love

and feel your presence,
    may be blessed by the gifts
        we have given this day. Amen.

Sending Forth

Benediction (Isaiah 40)
    Go forth upon wings like eagles.
    Soar with the hope of God's powerful love.
    Run the race that is set before you.
    For God runs with you, and strengthens you,
        every step of the way.

February 15, 2015

Transfiguration Sunday
Safiyah Fosua

Color

White

Scripture Readings

2 Kings 2:1-12; Psalm 50:1-6; 2 Corinthians 4:3-6; Mark 9:2-9

Theme Ideas

The one thing that Elisha and the three disciples have in common is the grace of attentiveness to the presence and activity of God. God is actively at work around us. Will we have eyes to see the glory of God?

Invitation and Gathering

Contemporary Gathering Words (2 Kings 2, Mark 9)
God calls us to leave the mundane valley,
    as we climb the mountain of God this day.
We climb with Peter, James, and John,
    who were granted a rare vision
    of the glory of God in Christ.

We climb with Elisha, who longed for a blessing
    in that split-second moment
    when heaven and earth intersected
    as Elijah was carried away.
May we experience a similar intersection today,
    in this time and place. Amen.

Call to Worship (Mark 9)

God calls us to the mountaintop.
    God, we come!
Christ invites us to the place where the Spirit's presence
is revealed in power and glory.
    God, we are here!
The Spirit offers us a revelation of the Living Lord
    As we worship this day,
        open our eyes to your presence, O God,
        and transfigure our lives
        to mirror your own!
Amen.
    Amen!

Opening Prayer (2 Kings 2, Mark 9)

God, open our eyes to experience your glory.
Make us like Peter, James, and John,
    who left daily life behind
        as they climbed your mountain
           to touch the divine.
Make us like Elisha,
    who refused to leave his mentor and teacher Elijah
        in pursuit of a special blessing.
May we, who are gathered here today,
    be doubly blest by your presence with us,
        in all your power and glory,
           on this Transfiguration Sunday. Amen.

Proclamation and Response

Prayer of Confession (Mark 9)
Merciful God,
>we would rather envision you in our own image,
>>than catch a glimpse of you
>>>in your splendor and glory;
>we would rather imagine ourselves
>>as the center of the universe,
>>>than allow your vision
>>>>to show us things as they truly are.
Forgive us, O God,
>when we shut our eyes to your self-revelation
>>and insist that you look and behave just like us.
Forgive, Holy One, when our egos prevent us
>from seeing who you really are.

Words of Assurance (2 Corinthians 4:6)
The God who said, "Let light shine out of darkness,"
>brings light to the hidden areas of our souls
>and forgiveness to those who ask for it.
In the name of Jesus Christ, you are forgiven.

Passing the Peace of Christ
Christ's light shines in the darkness, illuminating the glory and splendor of our God. Let us share this light and glory as we exchange signs of the peace of Christ. (B. J. Beu)

Response to the Word (Mark 9)
God of grace and glory,
>we long to see who you really are
>>beyond the images we have invented
>>>for our convenience—

images borrowed of old
Reveal your holy presence to us once more,
and make us fit to see your glory. Amen.

Thanksgiving and Communion

Offering Prayer (2 Corinthians 4)
God, we humbly offer these gifts into your service
as we proclaim your good news
to those whose eyes are yet veiled.
In our living and in our giving,
help us proclaim Jesus Christ as Lord. Amen.

Sending Forth

Benediction (Mark 9)
It is not enough to visit the mountain,
or even to see Christ transfigured
with dazzling clothes.
Such moments remain a secret and a mystery
if they are not shared.
Go, now, in the love of God,
to bring light to a world
that dwells yet in the shadows.
Go, now, with the peace of God,
to bring a vision of joy and hope
to those who have lost their way. Amen.

February 18, 2015

Ash Wednesday
Mary J. Scifres

Color

Purple

Scripture Readings

Joel 2:1-2, 12-17; Psalm 51:1-17; 2 Corinthians 5:20b–6:10; Matthew 6:1-6:16-21

Theme Ideas

Renewing our spirits and returning to God reconnects our hearts to the heart of Christ. Today's worship is a time for spiritual renewal, based on honest reflection and introspection, in the hope that we may purge those things (memories, attitudes, past actions, current behaviors) that separate us from God. From this honest reflection, we confess and empty ourselves of our sins, so that God may refill and refuel our spirits with love, mercy, and grace. *(Editor's note: This order of service varies slightly from the pattern used in this resource.)*

Invitation and Gathering

Contemporary Gathering Words (Joel 2, Psalm 51)

Ashes and dust, sorrows and sins,
storm clouds and gloom...
This day is often mantled with a sense of gray.
Yet gray gives way to grace when we allow Christ
to breathe new life into our tired lives.
Come, let us open our hearts to God's mercy and love.

Call to Worship (Joel 2)

Gather the people, young ones and old,
for all are welcome here.
Blow the trumpet, sound the alarm,
for God is present now!
Bless this worship and the holy season before us,
for God calls us to this time and place.
Return, refocus, remember, renew,
for God invites us to join hearts and lives.

Opening Prayer (Joel 2, Psalm 51)

Holy God, bring your heart of love
into our time of worship.
Speak to our hearts,
that we may join with your love.
Renew your Spirit within us,
that our spirits may be wholly yours.
Focus our lives,
that we may again know the joy
of living in your grace
and abiding in your merciful love. Amen.

Proclamation and Response

Introduction to the Word (Joel 2, Psalm 51, Matthew 6)
Listen for solemn words of warning.
Listen for wisdom and truth.
But listen also for God's joy and gladness.
For where God's heart is, there God's treasure is,
 and God's heart is with us all.

Response to the Word (Psalm 51, Matthew 6)
Teach us wisdom
 in the secret places of our hearts, O God.
Speak truth to our spirits,
 that we may honestly face the demons and sins
  that separate us from the abundant love
   you offer us each day.
Hear our prayers,
 that we may return to you
  and be restored to the joy
   of your forgiveness and grace.

Prayer of Confession (Joel 2, Psalm 51)
Have mercy on us, O God.
 Grant us your love and grace.
You know the storms of our lives, the clouds of our sin,
the gloom of our sorrow.
 Grant us your love and grace.
Return to us now. Gather us in.
 Grant us your love and grace.

Time of Reflection
The trumpet sounds, not for glory or notice,
 but to call us to God's love and grace.
We are gathered in worship, not for publicity or praise,

but to remember our need for grace.
We are called to pray, not for appearance or show,
    but for a renewed spirit and a heart of love.
Let us pray silently:
    for grace where we are in need of love,
(Silence)
    for forgiveness where we have sinned,
(Silence)
    for renewal where our spirits are dying,
(Silence)
    for restoration where we are disconnected
        from the vine of life.
(Silence)

Invitation to the Imposition of Ashes
As you are ready, come forward to receive a blessing of ashes. May these ashes be a symbol of our willingness to put to death all the things that are killing us.

Words of Blessing (As People Receive Their Ashes)
From the ashes, receive anew God's Easter promise of mercy and love.

Words of Assurance (Joel 2, Psalm 51)
God is grace and mercy, forgiveness and love.
God's anger is slow, but God's love is swifter
    than arrows and deeper than the sea.
Love and forgiveness are ours this day.
    Love and forgiveness are ours this day.

Passing the Peace of Christ (Joel 2)
Bless this assembly with signs of forgiveness and love.
Share together the peace of God.

Thanksgiving and Sending Forth

Offering Prayer (Matthew 6)
    Merciful God, we offer our lives to you [this night],
        that we may again be your people—
            a people restored by your mercy and grace.
    We offer our gifts and our tithes,
        that the treasures of this earth
            might not hold us back from our true treasure—
            our loving connection with you.
    Receive our gifts. Restore our lives.
    For you are the treasure we most need.

Invitation to the Offering and Benediction (Matthew 6)
    (Consider placing offering baskets at each door rather than gathering the plates during the service.)
    As you leave this place,
        share your alms and offerings quietly and in secret,
        that God may bless others with the gifts
        of your love and grace.
    As you go forth in the world,
        share your love quietly and abundantly,
        that God may bless others with the gifts
        of your love and grace.

February 22, 2015

B. J. Beu

Color

Purple

Scripture Readings

Genesis 9:8-17; Psalm 25:1-10; 1 Peter 3:18-22; Mark 1:9-15

Theme Ideas

On this first Sunday in Lent, we revisit Jesus' baptism against the backdrop of covenant, mercy, and salvation. In Genesis, God makes an everlasting covenant with Noah, his family, and every living creature. As a sign of God's promise to never again destroy all flesh with a flood, God set a rainbow in the sky. The psalmist seeks God's mercy and protection, truth and teachings. Extolling God's salvation, the psalmist proclaims God's steadfast love and faithfulness for all who keep God's covenant and decrees. The epistle hearkens to the flood of Noah, and to the salvation offered through the waters of Christ's baptism. Finally, the Gospel recounts John's baptism of Jesus and the beginning of Christ's ministry to spread the good news that God's kingdom has come near.

Invitation and Gathering

Contemporary Gathering Words (Genesis 9, Psalm 25, Mark 1)

In life and death, baptism and flood…
come to be washed in the waters of God.
From hunger and torment, demons and wild beasts…
leave the wilderness of your lives.
With grace and mercy, forgiveness and compassion…
prepare to meet the one who loves us.

Call to Worship (Genesis 9, Psalm 25, Mark 1:11)

A rainbow of grace paints the sky.
**We worship a God of steadfast love
and faithfulness.**
The bright ribbon of color serves to remind us…
**We worship a God of steadfast love
and faithfulness.**
The waters of baptism seal us in holy love.
**We worship a God of steadfast love
and faithfulness.**
A voice over the water proclaims:
"You are my Son, the Beloved;
with you I am well pleased."
**We worship a God of steadfast love
and faithfulness.**

Opening Prayer (Genesis 9, Psalm 25, 1 Peter 3, Mark 1)

Painter of rainbows amidst the clouds,
set your bow once more in the sky,

and remind us that your love and mercy
        are far greater than your righteous anger.
As we enter the season of Lent,
    remind us anew of your saving grace,
    and of our chance for rebirth,
        through the cleansing waters
            of our baptism.
Amidst the storms and floods of life,
    teach us the ways of life and death,
    that we may use this season
        as a time of gratitude for the past,
            and a time of hope for the future,
                through Christ our Lord. Amen.

Proclamation and Response

Prayer of Confession (Genesis 9, Psalm 25, 1 Peter 3, Mark 1)
Divine Spirit,
    you drive us into the wilderness of our lives.
In the solitude of our desert experiences:
    our thoughts rage out of control;
    our fears transform minor hills and obstacles
        into insurmountable mountains
        and impenetrable terrain;
    our sleep descends into nightmares
        that threaten to overwhelm us.
Renew us in the healing waters of our baptism,
    and send your angels to minister to us,
        that we may know that we are not alone.
Set your bow in the clouds once more, Holy Dove,
    that we might see the sign of your grace,
        and behold the promise of your salvation. Amen.

Words of Assurance (1 Peter 3, Mark 1:14)
> Hear and believe the good news: "The time is fulfilled,
>> and the kingdom of God has come near;
>> repent and believe in the good news."
> The one seated at the right hand of God
>> offers us forgiveness of sins and fullness of grace.

Passing the Peace of Christ (Psalm 25)
> God leads the humble on right paths and blesses the upright in heart with mercy and peace. Let us share signs of this peace and hope as we pass the peace of Christ.

Introduction to the Word (Psalm 25:10)
> As we listen for the word of God, let us remember that steadfast love and faithfulness are the paths of the Lord for those who keep God's covenant.

Response to the Word (Psalm 25:5)
> Make known your ways, O Lord.
> **Teach us your paths.**
> Lead us in your truth, and teach us, Holy One,
> **for you are the God of our salvation.**
> Make known your ways, O Lord.
> **Teach us your paths.**

Thanksgiving and Communion

Invitation to the Offering (Genesis 9, Mark 1)
> The One who saved Noah from the flood, the One who spoke words of approval for Jesus at his baptism, is full of mercy and steadfast love. In gratitude for our baptism and for our acceptance into God's family, let us be generous as we collect today's offering.

Offering Prayer (Genesis 9)
God of radical grace,
when we see your rainbow in the sky
after a winter storm,
we remember your covenant with us
and offer you our gratitude and praise.
For the many gifts of your creation,
we give you humble thanks.
May the gifts that we bring this day,
be a sign of our commitment
to share your love and mercy
with those in need.
In Christ's name, we pray. Amen.

Sending Forth

Benediction (Genesis 9)
Go forth as signs of God's love.
We go as rainbows of compassion and hope.
Go forth as children of God's promise.
We go as signs of God's love and mercy!
Go forth as heirs of God's covenant of grace.
We go as pools of baptismal water,
blessing all we touch.

March 1, 2015

Second Sunday in Lent
Laura Jaquith Bartlett

Color

Purple

Scripture Readings

Genesis 17:1-7, 15-16; Psalm 22:23-31; Romans 4:13-25; Mark 8:31-38

Theme Ideas

Following Jesus is not about a specific set of beliefs, it is simply about faith. Peter held certain beliefs about how the Messiah would act, but Jesus tells him clearly that he's got it all wrong. Peter is not alone. The truth is, most of us get it wrong. We try so hard to believe, but we lose hope when logic gets in the way. From the unbelievable story of Abram and Sarai getting pregnant late in life to the amazingly good news of the incarnate Son of God, these scriptures offer us hope upon hope upon hope. All we need is faith.

Invitation and Gathering

Contemporary Gathering Words (Genesis 17, Romans 4)
Gather together, all who are as good as dead.
Gather together, all who are beyond hope.
Gather together, all who have made mistakes.
Gather together, all who seek God's promises.
We have been gathered together by God.
We have been blessed by the Holy One!

Call to Worship (Psalm 22)
All who revere the Lord...
Praise God!
All who are Jacob's descendants...
Honor God!
All who are Israel's offspring...
Stand in awe of God!
All who have come to [name of your church]...
Worship God today!

Opening Prayer (Genesis 17, Romans 4)
God of Abram and Sarai,
you offered the hope and promise of a blessing—
a child of their own late in life,
a child of their own when nothing on earth
pointed to an abundant future.
You transform lives and shower grace
upon all generations.
God of Abraham and Sarah,
through your servants
you show us what faith looks like.
Help us give up our dependence on worldly logic,
that we may rest fully in your promise of new life.
Amen.

Proclamation and Response

Prayer of Confession (Genesis 17, Romans 4)
>Dear God, when we try to legislate your love
>>with policies and dogma, forgive us.
>Help us resist the temptation
>>to dismiss the miracles all around us,
>>>because they seem hard to believe.
>Forgive us, O God, and strengthen our faith.
>In Abraham and Sarah,
>>you have given us models of faith.
>Like them, empower us to be fully convinced
>>that you are able to do
>>>all that you have promised.
>Even in the face of death,
>>you do not desert us.
>Forgive our doubts,
>>and free us to rest secure in our faith. Amen.

Words of Assurance (Romans 4)
>Our lives are in the hands of the One
>>who raised Jesus from the dead.
>Rest assured that God's promise of abundant love
>>will never be forgotten!

Response to the Word (Genesis 17, Romans 4, Mark 8)
>When we don't know what to believe…
>>**God, give us faith.**
>When we judge others based on what they believe…
>>**God, give us faith.**
>When we fail to understand what it means
>to follow Jesus…
>>**God, give us faith.**

When we face despair, when we see no future,
when the cross looms ahead...
God, give us faith.
When we fail to remember your promise of resurrection,
and we deny our identity as an Easter people...
God, give us faith.

Thanksgiving and Communion

Offering Prayer (Genesis 17, Romans 4)
You have been faithful to your people, O God,
    from generation to generation.
Through the years,
    you continually shower us
        with your love and blessings.
Out of your abundance,
    we now share these blessings
        with those in need.
We give, not to prove our faith,
    but because our faith empowers us
        to live fully and generously. Amen.

Prayer after Communion
God of the ages,
    we lift up our hearts in grateful praise
        for your abundant grace
            and the hope we find
                in this sacred feast.
Just as you provided manna in the wilderness
    to your people long ago,
        you have given us your very self
            to feed us this day.
May this meal nourish our faith,

that we might go from your table
to give our very selves in service
to our sisters and brothers.
In the name of your Son, Jesus Christ, we pray. Amen.

Sending Forth

Benediction (Genesis 17, Mark 8)
*(If both a deacon and an elder are leading worship, the elder
would speak the first three lines, and the deacon would offer
the final line.)*
Go in faith to live God's promises.
Go in faith to follow Jesus Christ.
Go in faith to be sustained by the Holy Spirit.
Go in faith to serve God and your neighbor. Amen.

March 8, 2015

Third Sunday in Lent
Bill Hoppe

Color

Purple

Scripture Readings

Exodus 20:1-17; Psalm 19; 1 Corinthians 1:18-25; John 2:13-22

Theme Ideas

The nature of God's word is far beyond all human understanding. How can we possibly comprehend the act of creation when the Lord spoke and all that exists came into being? Yet for all its mystery and majesty, God's word is equally personal and intimate, and is to be lived in our lives: law and wisdom (Exodus 20 and 1 Corinthians 1), action and power (John 2 and Psalm 19), treasure, life, and ultimately love.

Invitation and Gathering

Contemporary Gathering Words (Psalm 19)
The law of the Lord is perfect.
The decrees of the Lord are sure!

The precepts of the Lord are right.
The commandment of the Lord is clear!
The fear of the Lord is pure.
The ordinances of the Lord are righteous and true!

Call to Worship (Psalm 19)
The heavens shout out the glories of the Lord.
God's handiwork is written across the skies.
The music of creation sings throughout the earth.
Day by day, night by night, in word and in song,
declare the glories of the Lord!

Opening Prayer (Exodus 20, John 2)
Lord, as we gather together in your house,
    we leave the ways of the world
        and all of its distractions behind.
We seek only to worship you in spirit and in truth,
    letting nothing come between us.
We want only to be enriched by your wisdom,
    your strength, your ways, and your love.
Bless all who have come to seek you,
    on this, your holy day. Amen.

Proclamation and Response

Prayer of Confession (Exodus 20, John 2)
Holy One, we profess to live
    according to your word and your commandments,
        yet we fill our lives in ways
            that prevent us from doing so.
Instead of making a temple of our hearts,
    where we would have you dwell,
        we have created a place of sickness, disease,
            and desires that lead to death.

Our hearts to become impure and false—
    a place where we have stolen, coveted, lied,
        and given our worship to false idols.
Cleanse and reclaim our hearts, Lord,
    as you cleansed the Temple in Jerusalem.
Overturn the tables in our spirit,
    and sweep aside all that keeps us from you.
Show us your steadfast love and forgiveness,
    as we seek to follow you once more. Amen.

Words of Assurance (John 2)

Jesus cleansed the Temple to save us
    from falsehood and deceit.
Jesus is still cleansing the temple of our lives,
    that we might be truly free to worship God
    in spirit and in truth.
(B. J. Beu)

Introduction to the Word or Prayer of Preparation (Psalm 19)

May the words I speak and may my innermost thoughts,
    be acceptable in your sight, Lord.
May they be pleasing to you—
    for you are my strength, my rock, and my Savior.

Response to the Word (Psalm 19)

The word of the Lord revives our souls.
The Lord's instruction makes our hearts rejoice!
God's word gives light to our eyes
    and makes our path clear.
The Lord's word is pure and righteous, eternal and true.
The word of God never fails!

—Or—

Response to the Word (1 Corinthians 1)
Lord, your wisdom and your ways
     defy worldly logic.
You have shown all of our knowledge and learning
     to be foolish in comparison.
How impossible it is to rationalize
     the means of our salvation,
          yet how simple it seems when we yield to faith.
How ridiculous the way of the cross seems to this world,
     and yet how powerful,
          when we choose to truly follow Christ.
If there is divine folly, it is wiser than we know.
If there is divine weakness,
     it is stronger than human strength.
Holy One, we are so foolish.
Become our wisdom,
     and become our strength. Amen.

Thanksgiving and Communion

Offering Prayer (Exodus 20)
Lord, you keep faith with untold thousands,
     with all who love you
          and keep your commandments.
How grateful we are for all that you have given us.
How thankful we are for your care to us,
     in matters large and small.
All that we can offer you in return is ourselves.
Receive our heartfelt love and worship. Amen.

Sending Forth

Benediction (Exodus 20, Psalm 19, 1 Corinthians 1)
The One who spoke creation into being,
who ordained the course of the stars and planets,
who makes the wise to become simple
and the simple to become wise,
who has given us the words of life,
and who is the living word,
goes with you—
to guide your steps,
to prepare the way for you,
to inhabit each and every breath you take,
and to live through you and within you.
All praise and glory and honor to our Lord! Amen!

March 15, 2015

Fourth Sunday in Lent/One Great Hour of Sharing

Karin Ellis

Color

Purple

Scripture Readings

Numbers 21:4-9; Psalm 107:1-3, 17-22; Ephesians 2:1-10; John 3:14-21

Theme Ideas

On this Fourth Sunday in Lent, themes of redemption, grace, mercy, and steadfast love abound. We give thanks for God's steadfast love, abounding mercy, and the endless grace that fill our lives. And we acknowledge Christ, who is the Son of God, as our light in the darkness. In the passage from Numbers, we remember that God's people have always complained, have always forgotten the providence of God, and have always turned away. But God never forgets, and God never turns away from us. The psalmist calls the people to gather, remembering God's saving and healing powers, and offering thanksgiving and praise. The letter to the Ephesians reminds

56

us that even though our lives might be marked by sin, grace is a gift from God—a gift that allows us to be faithful followers of Christ. And who is this Christ? John proclaims Christ to be the Son of God, the one who was sent to the world out of love.

Invitation and Gathering

Contemporary Gathering Words (Psalm 107)
From the east and the west,
from the north and the south,
we come to dwell in God's steadfast love.
God's love heals, forgives,
and welcomes all!

Call to Worship (Psalm 107, Ephesians 2)
We are God's people, gathered from many places,
to give thanks and to proclaim God's steadfast love.
This gift of love has no end.
We receive this gift with open hearts and open hands.
We are ready to worship and to serve.

Opening Prayer (Ephesians 2, John 3)
Gracious and loving God,
we have come to this place
to be your faithful disciples.
On this Lenten journey,
help us grow in our faith
and in our relationship with you.
Open our hearts to your love.
Open our eyes to the light of your Son.
Open our hands to the work of your Holy Spirit.

Help us share your grace
    and follow the ways that lead to new life.
In the name of Christ, we pray. Amen.

Proclamation and Response

Prayer of Confession (Ephesians 2, John 3)
God of grace and mercy,
    Lent is often a difficult time for us.
Our relationship with you is not what it could be.
Following Jesus is hard work,
    and sin clings to our lives—
        breaking our relationships with one another,
        leading us away from you.
Forgive us and help us turn back to you.
May we walk this Lenten journey
    with you and with Christ,
        knowing it is Christ who redeems,
            forgives, and heals.
May we follow the light of life,
    the source of love. Amen.

Words of Assurance (Ephesians 2)
Brothers and sisters, God is rich in mercy,
    making us alive together in fellowship with Christ.
By grace we have been saved.
Receive forgiveness and live in abundant love!

Passing the Peace of Christ
God has gathered us here in this place. In thanksgiving
for all God has done, let us greet one another with signs
of the peace of Christ.

Introduction to the Word

The Word of God beckons us.
The Spirit of God empowers us.
May we hear and receive this day,
all that God has to share with us.

Response to the Word (Numbers 21, Ephesians 2, John 3)

Holy One, since the beginning of time,
you have been creating and redeeming,
sustaining and healing,
all of creation.
In your mercy, you have brought forth possibilities
of new life within your people.
Help us respond to your great gifts
by offering forgiveness and healing,
and by sharing the light of Christ
with those we meet.
Empower us for the ministry that lies ahead,
in the name of Christ, our Lord. Amen.

Thanksgiving and Communion

Invitation to the Offering (Psalm 107)

The psalmist implores us to "offer thanksgiving sacrifices." May the gifts we offer today be symbols of our gratitude for God's love and blessings.

Offering Prayer (Psalm 107)

Merciful God, we give you thanks and praise
for all that you have given us.
Help us share your deeds, with songs of great joy,
even as we offer the gifts we bring this day
to help your children throughout the world.
Amen.

Sending Forth

Benediction
Brothers and Sisters, go from this place
knowing that you are loved and forgiven.
Go in peace. Amen.

March 22, 2015

Fifth Sunday in Lent

B. J. Beu

Color

Purple

Scripture Readings

Jeremiah 31:31-34; Psalm 51:1-12; Hebrews 5:5-10; John 12:20-33

Theme Ideas

We worship a God of renewal. The prophet Jeremiah proclaims that the days are surely coming when God will make a new covenant with Israel—a covenant written on the heart, not on parchment. The psalmist declares that God will put a new and right spirit within us. Jesus proclaims that renewal is neither easy nor free, but requires sacrifice, even death. For unless a grain of wheat dies and is buried, it yields no fruit. The author of Hebrews says that Christ has made the sacrifice necessary for this renewal in our lives.

Invitation and Gathering

Contemporary Gathering Words (Psalm 51)
>Are you feeling tired and worn out?
>>**Call on the name of the Lord.**
>Are past mistakes weighing heavily upon you?
>>**Come to the fount of living waters.**
>Are you the person you wish to be?
>>**Seek God's help, and it shall be granted you.**
>Are you looking for a better path?
>>**Ask Christ to show you the way.**

Call to Worship (Jeremiah 31, Psalm 51:10-12)
>If you need a fresh start, make your need known:
>>**"Create in me a clean heart, O God,**
>>**and put a new and right spirit within me."**
>If you feel far from God, call out in your need:
>>**"Cast me not away from your presence,**
>>**and take not your Holy Spirit from me."**
>If the cares of the world hang about your neck,
>plead to the Lord with all your might:
>>**"Restore to me the joy of my salvation,**
>>**and uphold me with a willing spirit."**
>If you need a fresh start, turn to God,
>for God will hear your prayers.

Opening Prayer (John 12)
>God of the unknown,
>>our souls are troubled
>>>until they find their rest in you.
>Afraid that we have not truly lived,
>>we fear our own mortality
>>>and the deaths of those dear to us.

Help us to face the future unafraid,
>   that we may know in the very marrow of our bones
>   the truth of Christ's words:
>   "Truly, truly, I say to you,
>   unless a grain of wheat
>   falls into the earth and dies,
>   it remains alone; but if it dies,
>   it bears much fruit."
In our living and in our dying,
>   renew us in the knowledge
>   that you are drawing all people to yourself.
>   Amen.

Proclamation and Response

Prayer of Confession (Jeremiah 31, Psalm 51:10-11)
God of infinite chances,
>   you are ever more ready to hear
>   than we are to pray;
>   you are ever more ready to offer forgiveness
>   than we are to seek it for ourselves,
>   or for others.
Create in us a clean heart, O God,
>   and put a new and right spirit within us.
For we are weighed down by the burden
>   of petty resentments and trivial slights
>   that poison our souls like toxic fumes.
Write your law on our hearts,
>   and take away our feeble protestations
>   that we know not what we do.
Do not cast us away from your presence,
>   and do not take your Holy Spirit from us.

Assurance of Pardon (Jeremiah 31, Psalm 51)

The One who loves us is faithful,
remembering our sins no more.
Look within and know that you are loved and accepted
by our gracious God.

Passing the Peace of Christ (Psalm 51)

We, who have received mercy, should offer mercy to others. With clean hearts and renewed spirits, let us rejoice in God's peace as we share the peace of Christ with one another.

Introduction to the Word (John 12)

Jesus prayed that God's name would be glorified, and it was glorified. As we prepare to hear God's word, let us pray that God may be glorified in the hearing and in the living of this, God's holy word.

Response to the Word (Jeremiah 31, John 12)

God writes the ways of life on our hearts.
Look inside you and trust that the truth of God's words
is written within.
Live as those whose hearts are pure
and whose love is deep.

Thanksgiving and Communion

Invitation to the Offering (Jeremiah 31, Psalm 51)

The One who writes the law of love on our hearts, the One who saves us from the worst parts of ourselves, is here to bless us once more. In giving we receive; in loving we find love bestowed upon us. In the spirit of Christian love, let us show our care for one another as we offer our tithes and offerings to God.

Offering Prayer (Jeremiah 31, Psalm 51, John 12)
> Nurturing God,
>> with hearts washed clean
>>> and spirits made new,
>>>> we celebrate the joy of your salvation.
>> Bless our tithes and offerings this day,
>>> that they may bear much fruit
>>>> in the lives of those who need it most. Amen.

Sending Forth

Benediction (John 12)
> Renewed in God, life is worth living again.
>> **In God, we bear much fruit.**
> Restored in Christ, death has lost its sting.
>> **In Christ, we are servants of God's sacred fire.**
> Reborn in the Spirit, hope is rekindled in the soul.
>> **In the Spirit, we are renewed and made whole.**
> Go with God's blessing.

March 29, 2015

Palm/Passion Sunday
Joanne Carlson Brown

Color
Purple

Palm Sunday Readings
Psalm 118:1-2, 19-29; Mark 11:1-11

Passion Sunday Readings
Isaiah 50:4-9a; Psalm 31:9-16; Philippians 2:5-11; Mark 14:1–15:47 or Mark 15:1-39 (40-47)

Theme Ideas
The long journey of Lent is over. We have reached Holy Week with its glorious beginning and tragic, painful end. With so much happening this week, it is impossible to cover it all. This is a day to convey the joy, the anger, the love, the betrayal, the struggle of souls trying to know what to do—a day to show or foreshadow the horrific ending no one in the story really expected. Our task is to help our people experience, in new and vital ways, an all-too-familiar story.

Invitation and Gathering

Contemporary Gathering Words (Mark 11)

One: Wow, this is great!

Two: Yeah, I love a parade.

One: Look, everyone is throwing their cloaks on the ground.

Two: I'm so excited, I just can't hold it in.

Both: Blessed be the one who is coming in our God's name!

All: Hosanna!

One: Now that's how to make an entrance.

Two: Let's go see what happens next.

Call to Worship (Mark 11, Psalm 118)

Give thanks to God,

whose steadfast love endures forever.

Give praise to the one who comes in God's name.

We wave our palms in praise and celebration.

This is the day that our God has made.

Let us rejoice and be glad. Hosanna!

Opening Prayer (Mark 11, 14–15; Psalm 118)

God of steadfast love,

we celebrate the coming of your Messiah

with glad songs and hosannas.

We wave our palms and cheer.

May we wholeheartedly celebrate the life,

the foreboding, and the love and grace

that this day symbolizes,

even while clouds gather on the horizon.

As we hear a familiar story told once more,

open our hearts to receive these words anew,

that they may shape our lives and faith. Amen.

Proclamation and Response

Prayer of Confession (Mark 11, 14–15)

Loving God, we sing and shout, "Hosanna!
> Blessed is the one who comes
>> in the name of the Lord!"
How easy it is to ignore what is to come—
> anger, betrayal, torture, and death.
Forgive us, Holy One,
> when we move from the celebration of Palm Sunday
>> to the celebration of Easter,
>>> without taking time to hear or experience
>>>> the passion and depths in between.
Forgive us for the times we have fallen short:
> when we have been the cause of anger
>> or been angry without cause;
> when we have betrayed the innocent;
> when we have stood by and condoned torture
>> in the name of national security;
> when we have rejoiced at the deaths
>> of those labeled terrorists, radicals,
>>> and insurrectionists.
Help us be faithful to your gospel of love
> and liberation.
Surround us with your enabling grace.
Bless us with a community
> to help us live a life of faithfulness—
>> faithfulness to the one who came to teach us
>>> how to live and how to love;
>> faithfulness to one for whom
>>> we are waving palms today. Amen.

Words of Assurance (Psalm 118)

"God's steadfast love endures forever."
This is not just a phrase from the psalmist.
It is not merely an abstract concept,
　　but a true and absolute reality and promise.
There is nothing we can do
　　to make God love us any less.
The gate is open for all who are heartily sorry,
　　who confess, and who try to live righteously.
Rejoice and be glad.

Passing the Peace of Christ (Mark 11)

Turn and greet the people around you with the words:
"Hosanna! Blessed be the one who comes in God's name!"
(Tickling them with a palm is permitted.)

Introduction to the Word (Psalm 118)

God is our rock and our fortress. We can rely on God to help us hear, not only words of celebration, but words of anguish—words that challenge us and distress us. May God open our ears, our eyes, and our hearts, to let these words in and bathe us with steadfast love.

Response to the Word (Mark 11, 14–15; Psalm 118)

For the chance to relive the last week of Jesus' life;
for the opportunity to bear witness to Jesus' passion;
for the love that surrounds us even in the difficult words,
we give you thanks, O God of steadfast love.

Thanksgiving and Communion

Invitation to the Offering (Mark 11, 14–15)

We have heard the story of celebration and challenge. This story, our story, calls forth a response from us—a response to give all of ourselves, and all that we can, in return for all that has been given to us. Our morning offering will now be received.

Offering Prayer (Mark 11, 14–15)
> We respond to your love
> > with love and gratitude, O God.
> We are touched by the story
> > of the one you sent to save us.
> In gratitude and thanks,
> > we dedicate this offering and our very selves
> > > to the ones you care so much about. Amen.

Sending Forth

Benediction (Mark 11, 14–15)
> We have gone from "Hosanna!" to "Crucify!"
> It has been a long and painful journey.
> Go forth, knowing that the story does not end here.
> The ending of the story is . . . to be continued!

April 2, 2015

Holy Thursday

Mary J. Scifres

Color

Purple

Scripture Readings

Exodus 12:1-4 (5-10), 11-14; Psalm 116:1-2, 12-19;
1 Corinthians 11:23-26; John 13:1-17, 31b-35

Theme Ideas

We are saved and served in order that we may serve. God saved the Hebrew people from slavery in Egypt so that they could fulfill their Abrahamic call to be "a light to the nations" and to become the people of God under Mosaic law. Jesus serves dinner to the disciples, then washes their feet to prepare them to serve one another and others under the new commandment of love. Even the remembrance of Christ, in our service of Holy Communion, is a means of nourishing our souls, so that we may go forth and serve as Christ's disciples. Remembering and reciting these ancient words, and participating in these ancient rituals, reminds us that we are saved and served by God, in order that we might serve God's world with love and mercy.

Invitation and Gathering

Contemporary Gathering Words (Exodus 12, 1 Corinthians 11, John 13)

(Each line may be printed or spoken with or without the response.)

On this night, we remember and reflect.

We have been saved in order to serve.

On this night, we wash and prepare.

We have been saved in order to serve.

On this night, we eat and rejoice.

We have been saved in order to serve.

On this night, we pray and grieve.

We have been saved in order to serve.

On this night, we remember and reflect.

We have been saved in order to serve.

Introduction to the Word (Exodus 12)

As the people gathered in Egypt, preparing to flee from the wrath of the Egyptians, so now we gather to remember and reflect. We gather to remember the ancient story of the Passover, and to reflect upon the final time Jesus shared the Passover meal with his disciples. *(Read Exodus 12:1-14 and John 13:1-2a)*

Call to Worship (Exodus 12, 1 Corinthians 11)

The table is prepared, the people are gathered.

We are ready to worship in spirit and in truth.

Opening Prayer (Exodus 12, 1 Corinthians 11, John 13)
>Loving God, we come into your presence
>>with gratitude and joy,
>>>even as we face memories
>>>>of sorrow and loss.
>We remember, with gratitude,
>>the traditions of our faith,
>>the ancient stories that bind us together,
>>and the people of God who lovingly served others,
>>>that we might know your saving love.
>Inspire us anew with the memory of that Passover meal
>>when Jesus shared his last night with his friends,
>>>offering himself in servanthood and love.
>In his holy name, we pray. Amen.

Proclamation and Response

Call to Confession (Psalm 116)
>Call upon the Lord, for God will surely hear your prayer.

Prayer of Confession (Psalm 116)
>God of grace and mercy,
>>save each and every one of us,
>>>that we may serve with confidence and love.
>Give heed to the prayers we bring before you now.
>*(A time of silent prayer may follow.)*
>Merciful God, release the ropes that bind us.
>Lift us from the fears that bury us.
>Save us from the troubles and trials
>>that separate us from you and from one another.
>Save us, O God, that we may serve the world
>>with confidence and love. Amen.

Words of Assurance (Exodus 12)

God has loosed our bonds
and saved us from slavery to sin and death.
Put on your sandals and gird your loins,
for God is calling us to lives of love and service!

Passing the Peace of Christ

As children of God, forgiven by grace and saved by love,
let us share signs of grace and love with one another.

Introduction to the Word (1 Corinthians 11)

We received a tradition from Christ—a tradition that
was handed down first by the disciples, then by Paul
and our church ancestors, and now by the beloved pastors and members of this church. (*Read 1 Corinthians
11:23-26*)

Thanksgiving and Communion

Invitation to Communion (1 Corinthians 11)

The table is prepared, the people are gathered.
We are ready to eat and to remember.
(*Service of Holy Communion—See* The Abingdon Worship
Annual 2013 *for a Great Thanksgiving related to these scrip-
tures and this service.*)

Introduction to the Word

Even at the final meal he would share with his disciples, Jesus knew that God had given everything into his
hands. Even in the face of impending death, Jesus knew
that he had come from God and was returning to God.
Even in the presence of disciples who would betray
and deny him, he offered himself as a holy and living

sacrifice. And so, in service and love, Jesus humbled himself by washing the feet of his friends and disciples. Hear now this beautiful story of love. *(Read John 13:4-17.)*

Invitation to the Offering and Service of Foot Washing (John 13)

The basin is prepared, the people are gathered.
We are ready to receive and remember.
As you come to receive this symbol of Christ's love, you are also invited to offer yourselves in loving sacrifice as you share your gifts to a world in need of Christ's mercy and love.
(Service of Foot Washing follows here. People may come forward to have feet or hands symbolically washed with a small pouring of water and gentle drying with a soft cloth or towel. Offering baskets or plates should be available at both the front and back.)

Offering Prayer After the Service of Foot Washing (John 13)

Loving Servant,
> we return thanks for washing our feet
>> and for bringing us into full fellowship
>>> with you and all God's people.

We offer you our very selves,
> that we may fulfill your law of love. Amen.

(B. J. Beu)

Sending Forth

Benediction (John 13)

Now Christ has been glorified,
and God has been glorified in Christ Jesus.
Little children, Christ who was with the disciples

for only a little while longer after this precious night,
remains with us always through the power
and the presence of God's Holy Spirit.
Even though we cannot yet go where Christ has gone,
we can receive and live this commandment,
newly given to his first disciples,
as they shared their last meal together:
Love one another.
> **Just as Christ has loved us,**
> **so we also must love one another.**
This is how everyone will know
> that we are Christ's disciples:
> **When we love one another**
> **as Christ has loved us.**
Go forth in love.

April 3, 2015

Good Friday
B. J. Beu

Color

None

Scripture Readings

Isaiah 52:13–53:12; Psalm 22; Hebrews 10:16-25; or 4:14-16; 5:7-9; John 18:1–19:42

Theme Ideas

Suffering, rejection, and loss focus our readings. Although Isaiah 52 begins with the exaltation of God's servant, it is a chilling reminder of how easily we turn on those God sends to help and save us. Psalm 22 poignantly expresses the sense of being abandoned by God. Jesus quotes from this psalm as he hangs on the cross. Peter's betrayal of his friend and teacher in the courtyard depicts just how low we can sink, and how far our betrayal can reach when events spiral out of our control—even for those we love. *(Worship Note: If your congregation has a gold or brass cross on its Lord's Table, substitute a rough-hewn wooden cross with horseshoe nails at the places of Jesus' hands and feet.)*

Invitation and Gathering

Contemporary Gathering Words (Hebrews 10)

The curtain has been thrown open.
Enter God's holy temple with reverence and awe.
This is Christ's doing.
It is marvelous in our sight.
The curtain has been thrown open.
Enter God's holy temple with reverence and awe.

Call to Worship (Isaiah 53)

Who would believe what we have heard?
God's servant grew up like a young plant.
Like a root out of dry ground
he grew up before the Lord of hosts.
Yet he was despised and rejected by others,
a man of suffering, acquainted with ridicule
and rejection.
We held him of no account,
as one stricken and struck down by God.
But he was wounded for our transgressions,
and crushed for our iniquities.
All we, like sheep, have gone astray.
We have all turned to our own way.
By a perversion of justice he was taken away.
Who could have imagined his future?
For he was cut off from the land of the living,
stricken for the transgressions of his people.
Out of his anguish, we shall see light.
The righteous one, God's servant,
shall make many righteous.
Who would believe what we have heard?

Opening Prayer (Psalm 22, John 18-19)
Fountain of tears,
>how it must have broken your heart
>>to behold the unspeakable cruelty
>>>your Son endured during his last days.
All these years later,
>as we retell the story of Jesus' passion:
>>our mouths dry up like broken pottery,
>>our hearts melt like wax within us,
>>our lives are poured out like water.
In our disbelief and dismay,
>help us face our emptiness
>>and know that you are always with us,
>>>even when your ways are beyond us,
>>>>and you remain shrouded in mystery.
Amen.

Proclamation and Response

Prayer of Confession (Isaiah 53, Psalm 22, John 18-19)
Merciful God,
>this is a night of long-forgotten hosannas,
>>a night of sleeping disciples
>>>and of betrayal with a kiss;
>this is a night of denials and scoffers,
>>a night of whips and of washing our hands
>>>to our culpability in evil;
>this is a night of thorns and nails,
>>a night of crying out with the psalmist:
>>>"My God, my God,
>>>>why have you forsaken me?";

this is a night when we glimpse human folly
and feel, in the marrow of our bones,
the depth of our own human frailty;
this is a night when we witness the razor's edge
separating hope and despair,
a night of acute awareness
of how often we stand mute and frozen
in the unfolding suffering of our world.

Assurance of Pardon (Isaiah 52, Hebrews 10)

Out of Christ's anguish, we shall see light.
Poured out to death, Christ makes intercession for us
and opens the curtain between us and the living God.

Passing the Peace of Christ (John 18)

Judas betrayed Jesus with a kiss, a sign of peace. Let
those of us who truly love Christ redeem Judas' betrayal
by offering one another signs of genuine Christian love
and peace on this holy day/night.

Introduction to the Word (Hebrews 10:16, NRSV)

Thus says the Lord: "This is the covenant that I will
make with them after those days: I will put my laws in
their hearts and I will write them on their minds." Listen for the word of God.

Response to the Word (Isaiah 52:15, 53:1)

Who can believe what we have heard?
The truth of God's Son will startle many nations.
Rulers will be silenced because of him;
for they will see what they have not seen,
and they shall hear and ponder
what they have not heard.
Can we do less?

Thanksgiving and Communion

Invitation to the Offering (Psalm 22, John 18-19)
> Let us pour ourselves out like water, that the gifts we
> offer may be worthy of the gift we have received from
> the one who poured out his life for us.

Offering Prayer (Isaiah 52, Psalm 22, Hebrews 10)
> God of infinite love and grace,
>> as you exalted and lifted up your Son,
>>> so may our gifts lift up your servants
>>>> who are hated and despised;
>> as your mercy has brought us healing,
>>> so may our offerings be used to heal others;
>> as your Son fed the poor until they were satisfied,
>>> so may our gifts tend to those in need. Amen.

Sending Forth

Benediction
> *(This is frequently omitted on Good Friday.)*
> In the midst of our pain and anguish,
>> rage, rage against the dying of the light.
> Hold fast to that flickering flame of hope
>> that struggles for life in the heart of the darkness.
> *(Drape the cross with black cloth and extinguish the Christ
> candle. Have rubrics in the program for the people to depart
> in silence.)*
> NOTE: Inspired by Dylan Thomas's "Do Not Go Gentle
> into That Good Night," from *The Poems of Dylan Thomas*
> (New Directions Publishing: 1939, 1946).

April 5, 2015

Easter Sunday
Mary J. Scifres

Color

White

Scripture Readings

Acts 10:34-43; Psalm 118:1-2, 14-24; 1 Corinthians 15:1-11; John 20:1-18 or Mark 16:1-8

Theme Ideas

Knowing and understanding pull today's scriptures into focus as we reflect on the mystery of death and resurrection. In John's Gospel, Mary does not know where Jesus' body has gone. Peter and the beloved disciple are confused about Jesus' teachings about his death and resurrection. In Mark's Gospel, Mary and the other women are startled and confused by the angel's appearance, and flee in terror and dread. But then Jesus calls Mary by name (John 20:16), and she finally recognizes her beloved teacher. With confidence, Peter reminds his listeners that they know Christ's message. Likewise, Paul reminds the church of Corinth to hold firmly to the message of Christ that they have received. As we know and understand, our eyes are opened and hope emerges. Faith grows, and life begins anew.

Invitation and Gathering

Contemporary Gathering Words (John 20)
(Begin the service in darkness. These gathering words may begin with the reading of John 20:1-12.)
Why are you weeping?
Whom are you seeking?
We don't know where to find Jesus.
The days have been dark.
The news has been sad.
We don't know what to do with our grief.
The cross has claimed his life.
The tomb has shrouded our hope.
We don't know where to turn for comfort.
Who has stolen him from us?
Why are we alone at the tomb?
We don't know where to look for answers.
Tears and sorrow blind us in our grief.
We don't know where to find Jesus.
(These gathering words may end with the reading of John 20:13-18.)

Call to Worship (1 Corinthians 15, John 20)
(Lights are gradually brightened, reaching full brightness at last line.)
Remember the good news that Jesus promised.
We will not be left alone.
Death cannot contain the purposes of God.
We will rise and live with this hope.

Tears and weeping will be no more.
We will know joy and laughter again.
This is the day that the Lord has made.
Let us rejoice and be glad in it.
Rejoice for Christ is risen.
Christ is risen indeed!
(Sing a joyous Easter hymn like "Christ the Lord Is Risen Today.")

Praise Sentences or Benediction
Christ is risen.
Christ is risen indeed!
Christ is risen.
Christ is risen indeed!

Opening Prayer (John 20)
Risen Christ, Lord of life,
breathe new life into us this day.
Inspire us with confidence,
and open our hearts anew,
to receive your promise of resurrection.
Speak to us once more,
that we might hear your voice
and recognize your presence in our midst.
From the darkness of doubt,
guide us into the glorious light
of faith and love.
In your holy name, we pray. Amen.

Proclamation and Response

Prayer of Confession
Lord of life,
you know our tears and our sorrows;

you know our doubts and our misgivings;
you know our sins and our shortcomings.
Heal us and strengthen us.
Forgive us and call to us now,
that we may leave the garden of despair
with the confidence that you walk with us
every step of the way. Amen.

Words of Assurance (Acts 10, Psalm 118, 1 Corinthians 15, Psalm 118)
Even as Christ died for our sins,
Christ rose to bring us newness of life.
Rise in the mercy and forgiveness of God.
Give thanks for God's steadfast love!

Passing the Peace of Christ (Psalm 118, 1 Corinthians 15)
Let us share the joy of our resurrection as we greet one another with love.

Introduction to the Word (John 20)
Why were you weeping? Whom are you seeking? Listen for the word of God and all your questions will be answered.

Response to the Word (Acts 10, Psalm 118, John 20)
Open the gates of your hope and truth, O God.
Open our ears to hear your voice,
when you call us by name.
Open our minds to recognize your presence,
as you walk beside us.
Live in us, that we may be signs of life and love
for a world shrouded in sorrow and fear.

Thanksgiving and Communion

Invitation to the Offering (Acts 10, John 20)
Let us offer signs of life and love, as we share our gifts
with God's world.

Offering Prayer (Acts 10, John 20)
With gratitude and joy, O God,
we bring forth these gifts
and ask for your blessing.
Live in and through these gifts
and the ministries of this church,
that we may bring new life
into a world ready to embrace the spring.

Sending Forth

Benediction (John 20)
Go into the world to share the good news.
We have seen Christ in our midst this day.
Go to sisters and brothers with the promise of hope.
**We rejoice and are glad in the knowledge
that Christ's promises are true.**

April 12, 2015

Second Sunday of Easter

Carol A. Cook Moore

[Copyright © 2014 by Carol A. Cook Moore.
Used by permission.]

Color

White

Scripture Readings

Acts 4:32-35; Psalm 133; 1 John 1:1–2:2; John 20:19-31

Theme Ideas

These scriptures overflow with witness to the resurrection of Jesus Christ. In the montage of witness stories, we find the unbelievable generosity of an early church community that echoes God's joy in unity. The Gospel contains even greater disbelief in the story of Thomas. This is a week to proclaim that doubt is a part of faith. Christ does what is needed so that we can see, touch, and taste the power of God. This power not only raises the dead, it empowers the believer to a life of conviction and generosity. Resurrection changes us.

Invitation and Gathering

Contemporary Gathering Words (1 John 1, John 20)
This is a place of resurrection joy. Come, hear, and see—
for new life is made real when we dare to share our
faith, and when we seek evidence of God's mercy and
love.

Call to Worship (1 John 1, John 20)
Behold, the resurrection claims us!
We want to see with our eyes
and touch with our hands
the marks of God's sacrificial love.
Behold, the Spirit calls to us!
We want to know the peace of those
who believe where they have not seen.
The ancestors sing to us: Christ is risen! God is light!
Live in this light!
Blessed are those who live the resurrection.
May we join their everlasting song: Alleluia!
Christ is risen indeed! Amen!

Opening Prayer (Acts 4, Psalm 133, 1 John 1, John 20)
Holy Lord, you are Light.
Grant us eyes to see and ears to hear
the resurrection joy so many cannot yet believe.
Open our hearts to hear the word
you proclaim to us this day.
Open our minds to embrace the life
you hold before us.
Show us the way of unity,
that we may live generously
as people of light.

Reign among us, resurrected one.
Reign in us today. Amen.

Proclamation and Response

Prayer of Confession (Acts 4, John 20)
Merciful God, we are humbled
    by the lives of the early disciples.
    We have forgotten how to face
        the cries of the needy,
            for there are so many.
    We have failed to place our trust
        in your sovereign love.
We have forsaken your demand for justice,
    at the expense of those who fight against darkness,
        each and every day.
    Forgive us, and all who claim to follow you.
    Fill us with your transforming Spirit,
        and free us with your grace,
            in the name of the risen one.
(A time of silent prayer may follow.)

Words of Assurance
Sisters and brothers, hear the good news:
    The love and mercy of God have been revealed
        in the cross and the empty tomb.
In the name of Jesus Christ, we are forgiven.
Live as reconciled people!
    Glory to God! Amen!

Passing the Peace of Christ
The peace that comes with God's grace is meant to
be shared. Let us share signs of this peace—a peace

available to us, right here, right now; a peace that brings new life in Christ.

Response to the Word (John 20)

Even though we have not seen the Lord,
we can still love him.
Even though we cannot touch his hands,
we can still believe.
Gathered here as the body of Christ,
and seeing Christ's love in one another,
we can say without doubt:
We have seen the Lord!
When we witness the hands that touch us,
and behold the eyes that shine with Christ's love and
        peace,
we can proclaim with faith:
My Lord and my God!
Do not doubt but believe.
(B. J. Beu)

Thanksgiving and Communion

Offering Prayer (Acts 4, John 20)

Holy Lord, your great grace is upon us.
Move us to proclaim with these gifts,
        that you are our Lord and our God.
Accept these offerings
        to your glory, honor, and praise. Amen.

Invitation to Communion

This is the food that opens our hearts to know the Risen Christ. This is the place where we are all welcome—whether we come with nagging doubts or with firm belief. For here God meets us with a love that is everlasting.

Sending Forth

Benediction (John 20)

Sisters and brothers, peace be with you.
In peace, go forth to proclaim God's love.
In peace, go forth and live as Christ's disciples,
that others may see your faith and also believe.
The love of God, the peace of Christ,
and the power of the Holy Spirit,
be with you now and forevermore. Amen.

April 19, 2015

Third Sunday of Easter
Karin Ellis

Color
White

Scripture Readings
Acts 3:12-19; Psalm 4; 1 John 3:1-7; Luke 24:36b-48

Theme Ideas
On this third Sunday of Easter, we continue to hear stories of resurrection and hope. Themes of repentance and righteousness flow through the psalm and the passage from 1 John. The psalmist assures us that the Lord hears our cries when we call out to God, and implores us to turn away from sin toward the God who puts gladness in our heart. First John offers a vision of hope, depicting a time when we will know what it means to be like Christ. While we wait for that time, we are called to turn away from sin, and seek righteousness. Encouraging us to repent and turn to God, Acts shares stories of healing and of receiving new life in the name of Jesus. In Luke's Gospel, Jesus makes a post-resurrection appearance amidst frightened and astonished disciples, proclaiming

peace, easing their fears, and reminding them to be witnesses "of these things." As we live a life of repentance, righteousness, and love, we can be witnesses of new life and seekers of resurrection moments.

Invitation and Gathering

Contemporary Gathering Words (Psalm 4)
In our desperation, we cry out:
"Where are you, God! We need you!"
When all hope seems lost,
God answers with love and mercy.
Praise be to God!

Call to Worship (Psalm 4)
People of God, the Lord has called you here today.
We have come seeking love, hope, and healing.
Rejoice, for the light of Christ shines on us.
Our hearts are full of gladness,
as we praise the One who promises new life!

Opening Prayer (Acts 3, Luke 24)
God of renewal, you are the Author of life.
You are the One who came to meet us
in flesh and bone and blood.
You are the One who walked among us,
proclaiming love, mercy, and repentance.
You are the One who died, and rose, and lived again,
that we might believe and truly live.
Empower us to be your witnesses
to the ends of the earth.
And help us accept your unconditional love,
that we might share your love with others.
In your holy name, we pray. Amen.

Proclamation and Response

Prayer of Confession (Acts 3, Luke 24)
God of grace,
>we have turned away from you
>>in so many ways.
Forgive us, Holy One:
>when we forget you;
>when we fail to recognize your works in this world;
>when we allow doubt to overcome our belief;
>when we allow fear to replace our trust and faith.
Help us remember that we are yours, your beloved.
As we turn to you, to receive your grace and mercy,
>bless us once more
>>that we may live lives of faithfulness. Amen.

Words of Assurance (1 John 3)
Brothers and sisters, God claims us as beloved children.
Receive God's forgiveness and rise with newness of life,
>born through the love of Christ.

Passing the Peace of Christ (Luke 24)
Jesus stood among his disciples and proclaimed, "Peace be with you." Brothers and sisters, turn and greet one another with the peace of Christ.

Introduction to the Word
May the words we hear
>be received with newness of life,
>>that we may go forth to love and to serve.

Response to the Word (Luke 24)
God, you know us better than we know ourselves.
May the words we have heard be printed on our hearts,

that we may be inspired, each and every day,
  to follow in the ways of Christ,
    and be witnesses of his resurrection. Amen.

Thanksgiving and Communion

Invitation to the Offering (Psalm 4)
God continues to be gracious to us, and blesses us with
many gifts and talents. We are asked to share these gifts,
and not hide them away. Let us bring our gifts to God
with open and glad hearts.

Offering Prayer
Almighty God, in this season of new life,
  we give you thanks and praise for these gifts.
May they be used
  to bring new life to others.
As we offer you our gifts,
  we offer you our hearts as well,
    knowing it is Christ who leads us
      and empowers us for ministry.
In your holy name, we pray. Amen.

Sending Forth

Benediction (Acts 3, Luke 24)
Friends, go forth into the world
  and be witnesses for Christ,
    sharing his love with everyone you meet.
Go in peace!

April 26, 2015

Fourth Sunday of Easter
B. J. Beu

[Copyright © 2014 by B. J. Beu. Used by permission.]

Color

White

Scripture Readings

Acts 4:5-12; Psalm 23; 1 John 3:16-24; John 10:11-18

Theme Ideas

The good shepherd and the shepherding love of Christ focus today's readings. While Acts focuses on the unique saving ability of Jesus Christ, John implies that other sheep are part of God's fold. The familiar words of Psalm 23 become fresh when interwoven with the words from John 10 and 1 John 3. Though not in today's readings, conjoining Psalm 23 with Isaiah 40:31 provides a vision of strength and comfort.

Invitation and Gathering

Contemporary Gathering Words (Acts 4, John 10)
(You may substitute "Christ" for "Jesus" in these Gathering Words.)

Who is the cornerstone of our faith?
Jesus is our cornerstone!
Who is our shepherd in these dark days?
Jesus is our shepherd!
Who can save us from this world of pain?
Jesus is our savior!

Call to Worship or Litany (Isaiah 40:31, Psalm 23, KJV)
Those who wait for the Lord shall renew their strength.
The Lord is my shepherd, I shall not want.
He makes me lie down in green pastures.
He leads me beside the still waters.
They shall mount up with wings like eagles.
He restores my soul.
He leads me in the paths of righteousness
for his name's sake.
They shall run and not be weary.
Yea though I walk through the valley
of the shadow of death, I shall fear no evil,
for thou art with me.
They shall walk and not faint.
Surely goodness and mercy shall follow me
all the days of my life, and I shall dwell
in the house of the Lord forever.

Opening Prayer (Psalm 23)
Shepherding God,
you bring us into your presence,
and shower us with your love.
You lead us beside still waters,
and restore our souls.
Touch our hearts and minds,
that we may live your love
and abide in your grace. Amen.

Proclamation and Response

Prayer of Confession (John 10, 1 John 3)
God of many pastures,
we never tire of hearing
the voice of our shepherd
calling us to lay our burdens down,
and to dwell in your house forever.
Forgive us, loving shepherd,
when we try to keep your care for ourselves alone—
believing that we have a special place
in your love;
thinking that others wander alone,
without your care and guidance.
Open our eyes to the other sheep in your fold,
wherever they might be,
and whatever they might look like. Amen.

Assurance of Pardon (Psalm 23)
The one who lays his life down for his sheep
will surely rescue us and lead us to safe pastures.
Through the love and grace of our shepherd,
goodness and mercy shall follow us
all the days of our lives,
and we shall dwell secure forever.

Response to the Word/Sermon (John 3)
Eternal God, our guide and guardian,
you call us to abide in your love,
and walk in your grace.
Help us live your love,
not only in our words,
but also in our deeds.

Enlighten our minds to your teachings,
    that we may be servants of your love.
Transform our church,
    that we may be shepherds
        of your grace. Amen.

Call to Prayer (Psalm 23)

Come, all who are weary and need rest. Come, all who thirst for springs that well up to eternal life. Come, all who hunger and thirst for righteousness. Lift up your prayers to our shepherd—the one who leads us through the valley of the shadow of death, the one who leads us into life.

Thanksgiving and Communion

Invitation to the Offering (John 10, 1 John 3)

The good shepherd calls us to love one another.
    We come, abiding in love.
The shepherd of love calls us to give of ourselves.
    We come, abiding in faith.
The shepherd of life calls us to be a blessing to others.
    We come, abiding in God's blessings.

Offering Prayer (John 10, 1 John 3)

Loving shepherd,
    as you have fed us in green pastures
        and led us beside still waters,
            so may our offering this day
                be a source of comfort and hope
                    to a world that needs a shepherd.

Sending Forth

Benediction (1 John 3)
Go forth in God's care,
taking love wherever you go.
We will abide in God's love.
Go forth in God's name,
taking Christ wherever you go.
We will abide in God's love.
Go forth in God's grace,
sharing mercy with everyone you meet.
We will abide in God's love.

May 3, 2015

Fifth Sunday of Easter
B. J. Beu

Color

White

Scripture Readings

Acts 8:26-40; Psalm 22:25-31; 1 John 4:7-21; John 15:1-8

Theme Ideas

God is love. Those who abide in love, abide in God. And those who abide in Christ's love, abide in Christ. For Christ is the vine and we are the branches. By abiding in the vine, we bear the fruit of love. Apart from the vine, we can do nothing. In Acts, Philip meets an Ethiopian eunuch and teaches him the meaning of Isaiah's suffering servant song, and helps him abide in the vine. The psalmist speaks of the servant who leads the people to abide in God. John writes that true love casts out fear and offers us Jesus' commandment to love one another. Truly, God is love. Those who abide in love, abide in God.

Invitation and Gathering

Contemporary Gathering Words (Psalm 22, 1 John 4)
> Touching love, we touch God.
> Showing mercy, we show Christ.
> Sharing abundance, we share the source of our hope.
> Worshiping God, we find ourselves.

Call to Worship (Acts 8, 1 John 4, John 15)
> Come to the household of love,
> for God is love.
> > **As we abide in love,**
> > **we abide in God.**
> Come to the vineyard of grace,
> for God is gracious.
> > **As we abide in the vine,**
> > **we bear the fruit of salvation.**
> Come bathe in baptismal waters,
> for God's Spirit awaits.
> > **As we abide in God's Spirit,**
> > **we abide in peace.**
> Come to the household of love,
> for God is love.
> > **Come! All are welcome here.**

Opening Prayer (John 15)
> Divine Vinegrower,
> > plant us in the soil of your love,
> > > for Christ is our vine
> > > > and we are the branches.
> In everything we say
> > and in everything we do,
> > > help us abide in the vine,

that we may bear the fruit
of your love and grace. Amen.

Proclamation and Response

Prayer of Confession (1 John 4, John 15)
Merciful One,
you teach us that perfect love casts out fear,
but we are often afraid;
you command us to love our sisters and brothers,
but we are often alienated from one another;
you invite us to abide in you as you abide in us,
but we often don't know how or where to begin.
Show us once more that abiding in your love
is as easy and natural as a branch
abiding in the vine.
Prune our imperfections,
that we may grow a heart so strong
that all our fears will be cast out,
leaving us ready and able
to abide in your great love.

Words of Assurance (John 15)
Christ is the vine, we are the branches.
If we abide in Christ; if we abide in the vine,
ask for grace and it will be given.
Abide in the vine and it is already given.

Passing the Peace of Christ (1 John 4:21)
This commandment we have from God: those who love
God ought to love their brother and sister also. Let us
show our love by exchanging signs of Christ's peace.

Introduction to the Word (Acts 8:30b)

Philip asked a foreigner reading from the scroll of Isaiah: "'Do you really understand what you are reading?' The man replied, 'Without someone to guide me, how could I?'" As we prepare to read today's scriptures, ask the Holy Spirit to be your guide. With the Spirit's help, listen for the word of God.

Response to the Word (John 15:7-8, NRSV)

Jesus makes us this promise: "If you abide in me, and my words abide in you, ask for whatever you wish, and it will be done for you. [God] my Father [Mother] is glorified by this, that you bear much fruit and become my disciples." As the people of God, and as branches that abide in the vine, let us glorify God together.

Thanksgiving and Communion

Invitation to the Offering (1 John 4)

To love God is to love people. No exceptions. No one who ignores the needs of the poor knows God. No one who hates another abides in God's love. Let us show our love for God as we offer our gifts, not only to Christ and Christ's church, but to the least and the last.

Offering Prayer (Psalm 22, 1 John 4, John 15)

Bountiful God,
>   you promise that the poor shall eat and be satisfied.
May your promise be fulfilled
>   through the gifts we bring to you this day.
Sanctify our offering,
>   that it may be for the world
>   a sign of your boundless love
>   and your overflowing abundance. Amen.

Invitation to Communion (1 John 4, John 15)
>Come to the table of grace,
>for Christ is the vine,
>and we are the branches.
>>**Come, Holy Spirit, come.**
>Come to the table of love,
>for whoever does not love,
>does not know God.
>>**Come, Holy Spirit, come.**
>Come to the table of blessing,
>for Christ is here to abide in us,
>as we abide in him.
>>**Come, Holy Spirit, come.**

Sending Forth

Benediction (1 John 4, John 15)
>Beloved, let us love one another,
>for love is from God.
>>**We will live with God's love in our hearts.**
>Beloved, let us abide in Christ's love,
>for he is the vine and we are the branches.
>>**We will grow as Christ's disciples in the world.**
>Beloved, let us care for one another,
>for the Spirit unites us together in compassion.
>>**We will share God's peace with one another.**

May 10, 2015

Sixth Sunday of Easter/
Festival of the Christian Home/Mother's Day
Amy B. Hunter

Color

White

Scripture Readings

Acts 10:44-48; Psalm 98; 1 John 5:1-6; John 15:9-17

Theme Ideas

It is still Easter! We are Easter people invited to trust
God faithfully and to love others fully. First John insists
that Christians cannot separate loving God from loving
Jesus—the one who lived, died, and was raised in the
flesh. John's Gospel tells us that we love God and remain true to Jesus only as we love one another. It is not
enough to love one another within our own communi-
ties and families, the power of the resurrection is not
content to stop there. The Holy Spirit sends Peter to the
Gentiles and insists that these "outsiders" are actually
part of the Christian family. In the book of Acts "Gentile
Pentecost," Peter ends up converted every bit as much
as his non-Jewish listeners are. Easter demands that we

live in God's ever-widening circle of love. Far from being the mascot of our faith community, or the household god of our particular family, God is Love, demanding from us an ever deeper and deeper loving response.

Invitation and Gathering

Contemporary Gathering Words (Psalm 98, John 15)
Sing joyful songs to God!
Alleluia! We are Easter people!
God has worked miracles!
Jesus is our joy!
Sing joyful songs to God!
Alleluia! We are Easter people!
God's love for us lasts forever.
Jesus makes us into friends.
Sing joyful songs to God!
Alleluia! We are Easter people!

Call to Worship (Acts 10, Psalm 98, John 15)
Alleluia! Even the ends of the earth
see the saving power of our God.
The sea roars with joy,
and the floods clap their hands.
Trumpets sound and horns celebrate with song!
Alleluia! The Holy Spirit falls upon all
who hear the word of God.
When God shows such generosity,
how can we withhold our love?
Alleluia! Jesus has extended to all people
the friendship of our God.
We were strangers and then servants,
but now we are God's friends.

Opening Prayer (Acts 10, John 15)
>   Holy God, you make us Easter people—
>   a people transformed by the resurrection
>   of your Son, Jesus.
>   Your first and final word to us is Love.
>   You reach out to us, offering joy and wholeness.
>   Yet we often greet your resurrection
>   by grieving at the tomb,
>   doubting the good news we hear,
>   or quaking in fear
>   as we hide in our upper rooms.
>   Still, you call us deeper into Easter,
>   answering our resistance
>   with your loving presence.
>   You claim us as your friends.
>   As we gather now to worship,
>   teach us once more to abide in your love,
>   that our joy may be complete. Amen.

Proclamation and Response

Prayer of Confession (Acts 10, Psalm 98, 1 John 5, John 15)
>   Lord Jesus Christ,
>   you reach across every boundary, even death itself,
>   and draw us into loving intimacy with you.
>   Forgive us for resisting your love.
>   You call us your friends,
>   yet we act like minor acquaintances
>   or even strangers.
>   You send us into the world to proclaim your love,
>   yet we gape in astonishment
>   when you include all people in your love.

The light of your resurrection
>> conquers the darkness in our lives,
>>>> yet we act as if your love is a burden.
>> Give us Easter lives, we pray,
>>>> for you alone have the power to save us. Amen.

Words of Assurance (1 John 5, John 15)
>> Jesus promises, "You did not choose me. I chose you."
>> We know that we are God's children,
>>>> raised to new life with Christ.
>> Abide in the saving love of Jesus Christ.

Passing the Peace of Christ (1 John 5, John 15)
>> Jesus loves us and gives us the grace to love one another. Greet one another with signs of the love and peace of the risen Christ.

Introduction to the Word (Acts 10, John 15)
>> The Holy Spirit falls on all who hear the word.
>> **Jesus, may your joy come fully alive in us**
>> **as we hear and obey your word.**

Response to the Word (Acts 10, John 15)
>> The Holy Spirit falls on all who hear the word of God.
>> **Jesus, we were strangers and servants,**
>> **but your word has made us friends.**

Thanksgiving and Communion

Invitation to the Offering (John 15)
>> Bring your offerings to God, and abide in the love and joy of the risen Christ.

Offering Prayer (John 15)

>God, you withhold nothing from us.
>You transform us with your friendship.
>You desire that we know and share your joy.
>We offer these gifts to you,
>>grateful for our Easter life in Jesus Christ.
>
>Use them, we pray,
>>to make your love and friendship
>>>known throughout the world. Amen.

Sending Forth

Benediction (Acts 10, Psalm 98, John 15)

>The whole creation celebrates God's victory of love.
>Live lives of victorious faith.
>>**When God shows such generosity,**
>>**How can we withhold our love?**
>
>Jesus abides in the love of God.
>Abide in God's love every day of your lives.
>>**When God shows such generosity,**
>>**How can we withhold our love?**
>
>Jesus calls you his friends.
>Carry the friendship of God to everyone you meet.
>>**When God shows such generosity,**
>>**How can we withhold our love?**

Benediction (Psalm 98, John 15)

>Alleluia! Alleluia! Let us go forth,
>bearing the fruit of God's love and joy.
>>**Thanks be to God! Alleluia! Alleluia!**

May 17, 2015

Ascension Sunday/Seventh Sunday of Easter
Deborah Sokolove

Color

White

Scripture Readings

ASCENSION SUNDAY: Acts 1:1-11; Psalm 47;
Ephesians 1:15-23; Luke 24:44-53
SEVENTH SUNDAY OF EASTER: Acts 1:15-17, 21-26;
Psalm 1; 1 John 5:9-13; John 17:6-19 *[Editors' Note: These
readings are included for reference. The liturgies and prayers
in this entry focus on the Ascension readings.]*

Theme Ideas

With the eyes of our hearts enlightened, we put our
faith in Jesus Christ, who was raised from the dead, and
whose body is the church. Proclaim repentance and forgiveness of sins in the name of Christ.

Invitation and Gathering

Contemporary Gathering Words (Psalm 47)
Clap your hands and shout to God
with loud songs of joy.

Sing praises to God, who fills the world
with forgiveness and grace.

Call to Worship (Acts 1, Psalm 47, Ephesians 1)
Christ is alive. He is risen from the dead.
The Holy One calls us to worship and praise.
Baptized with the power of the Holy Spirit,
we live with Christ in our hearts.
Clap your hands and shout to God
with loud songs of joy.
**Sing praises to God, who fills the world
with forgiveness and grace.**

Opening Prayer (Acts 1, Ephesians 1, Luke 24)
Blessed are you, Holy One,
creator of all that is and all that ever will be.
You sent your holy child, Jesus,
to heal us and bless us,
to show us your love.
After his suffering and death on the cross,
he was still among us,
proclaiming repentance and forgiveness of sins
for all who call on his name.
Just as you sent the power of the Holy Spirit
to those who first believed,
fill us now with your power and grace,
that we may become the hands and feet,
and heart and spirit, of Christ. Amen.

Proclamation and Response

Prayer of Confession (Acts 1, Luke 24)
Jesus said, "It is not for you to know the times
or periods that the Holy One has set."

Yet we keep searching for signs and omens,
trying to predict the future
instead of living fully each day.
Jesus said, "John baptized with water,
but you will be baptized with the Holy Spirit."
Yet we are more concerned
with following the proper procedures,
than with opening our hearts
to those around us.
Jesus said, "You will receive power
when the Holy Spirit has come upon you."
Forgive us, Holy One,
when we try to shape the world
according to our desires,
instead of asking for the power
to do your will.

Words of Assurance (Ephesians 1)
The Holy One enlightens the eyes of our hearts,
that we may know the hope to which we are called.
In the name of Christ, you are forgiven.
In the name of Christ, you are forgiven.
Glory to God.

Passing the Peace of Christ (Acts 1)
In the power of the Holy Spirit and the love of Christ, let
us share signs of peace with one another.
The peace of Christ be with you.
The peace of Christ be with you always.

Response to the Word (Ephesians 1)
With the eyes of our hearts enlightened,
we become witnesses to the glory of God.

Thanksgiving and Communion

Invitation to the Offering (Ephesians 1)
> Filled with the hope to which Christ has called us, let us
> lay our gifts and offerings at the foot of the cross.

Offering Prayer (Psalm 47, Ephesians 1)
> God of all creation, powerful Spirit, Savior of all,
>> use our gifts to bring hope to a world
>>> that is in need of your grace. Amen.

Great Thanksgiving
> Christ be with you.
>> **And also with you.**
> Lift up your hearts.
>> **We lift them up to God.**
> Let us give our thanks to the Holy One.
>> **It is right to give our thanks and praise.**

> It is a right, good, and a joyful thing,
>> always and everywhere, to give our thanks to you,
>> Holy One, our God, Maker of all that is,
>> and all that ever will be.
> We give you thanks for showing us your power
>> in the ancient stories of your people, Israel,
>> and in the new stories of hope
>> that are happening all around us.
> We give you thanks for revealing yourself to us
>> in your holy child, Jesus,
>>> for making us into members of his holy body,
>>> the church, and for calling us to witness
>>> to the power of your grace.

And so, with your creatures on earth
    and all the heavenly chorus,
    we praise your name and join their unending hymn:
    Holy, holy, holy Lord, God of power and might,
        heaven and earth are full of your glory.
    Hosanna in the highest. Blessed is the one
        who comes in the name of the Lord.
    Hosanna in the highest.
Holy are you, and holy is your child, Jesus Christ,
    who lived, died, and appeared again to his friends
    in Jerusalem, risen from the dead,
    telling them to proclaim repentance
    and the forgiveness of sins to all nations;
    and now lives in those who are called by his name.

On the night in which he gave himself up,
    Jesus took bread, gave thanks to you,
    broke the bread, and gave it to the disciples, saying:
    "Take, eat; this is my body which is given for you.
    Do this in remembrance of me."
When the supper was over, Jesus took the cup,
    offered thanks and gave it to the disciples, saying:
    "Drink from this, all of you;
    this is my life in the new covenant,
    poured out for you and for many,
    for the forgiveness of sins.
    Do this, as often as you drink it,
    in remembrance of me."
And so, in remembrance of your mighty acts
    in Jesus Christ, we proclaim the mystery of faith.
    Christ has died.
    Christ is risen.
    Christ will come again.

Pour out your Holy Spirit on us,
    and on these gifts of bread and wine.
Make them be for us the body and blood of Christ,
    that we may be the body of Christ
    to a world that yearns for joy.

God of all creation, powerful Spirit, Savior of all,
    we praise your holy, eternal, loving name. Amen.

Sending Forth

Benediction (Acts 1, Psalm 47, Ephesians 1, Luke 24)
    Go into the world, clothed with power from on high,
        carrying Christ's message of forgiveness and joy.
    The power of the Holy Spirit will go with you
        as you bear witness to this good news. Amen.

May 24, 2015

Pentecost Sunday
B. J. Beu

Color

Red

Scripture Readings

Acts 2:1-21; Psalm 104:24-34, 35b; Romans 8:22-27; John 15:26-27; 16:4b-15

Theme Ideas

As Jesus' disciples huddled together in fear, the Holy Spirit entered their dwelling in rushing wind and tongues of fire. From that event, the Church was born. We put on elaborate celebrations for Christmas and Easter, but Pentecost is equally important. Without Pentecost, the disciples would not have had the courage to go forth and spread the gospel. Without Pentecost, the Spirit promised to the prophet Joel would not be the active force it is in our world today: granting visions and dreams to our old and young alike. The power of God to create and renew life is the power of the Holy Spirit.

We see this power in the psalmist's hymn of praise. We behold this power in Paul's discussion of adoption in Christ through the Spirit. And we see the promise of this power in Jesus, as he comforts his disciples before his death.

Invitation and Gathering

Contemporary Gathering Words (Acts 2)
Close your eyes and pay attention to your breath.
The same Spirit that came on Pentecost in rushing wind
    resides in your breath.
Now feel the warmth of your body.
The same Spirit that came on Pentecost like holy fire
    warms your body.
Open your eyes and give thanks to the Holy Spirit,
    who is as near to us as our very breath.
Come! Let us worship.

Call to Worship (Acts 2, John 14)
In rushing wind, in cleansing fire…
    Come, Holy Spirit, come.
In courage found, in strength renewed…
    Come, Holy Spirit, come.
In visions born, in dreams restored…
    Come, Holy Spirit, come.
In hopes rekindled, in fears released…
    Come, Holy Spirit, come.
In the church's sudden birth, in possibilities untold…
    Come, Holy Spirit, come.
In rushing wind, in cleansing fire…
    Come, Holy Spirit, come.

Opening Prayer (Acts 2)
God of wind and flame,
    ignite a fire in our hearts
        on this day of Pentecost,
            and fill us with your courage and power.
Pour out your Holy Spirit
    on your people around the world,
        that our young people may have visions,
            and our elders may dream dreams.
Blow into our lives,
    and renew us as a people of faith,
        that we might spread the good news
            of your saving love,
                through Jesus Christ, our Lord. Amen.

Proclamation and Response

Prayer of Confession (Acts 2, Psalm 104, Romans 8)
Loving Father,
    you breathe life into our bodies
        and open your hand to fill us with good things,
            yet we act as if the world is against us.
Caring Mother,
    you dance with us upon the mountaintop
        and call us to sing and rejoice in your presence,
            yet we act as if we are little more than dust.
Spirit of gentleness,
    you come to us in our weakness,
        and intercede on our behalf
            with sighs too deep for words,
                yet we act as if we bear our burdens alone.

Come once more in rushing wind and cleansing fire,
>that we may open our eyes
>>to the glory of your world.
Through your Spirit, who shows us the way,
>open our ears to the needs of your people. Amen.

Words of Assurance (Psalm 104, Romans 8)

God searches the heart,
>and the Spirit helps us in our weakness.
For the Spirit intercedes for us
>according to the will of God.
Rejoice, sisters and brothers,
>for God's steadfast love endures forever.

Passing the Peace of Christ (John 15)

God has sent us the Holy Spirit, the Advocate, to bless us and save us from our fears. In celebration of this gift, let us share God's love with one another as we exchange signs of Christ's peace.

Introduction to the Word (Acts 2)

From a locked room, the disciples emerged to share their faith—a faith so deep it changed the world and birthed the church. As we listen for the word of God, may we hear with ears and hearts aflame with the power of the Holy Spirit.

Response to the Word (Romans 8)

All who are led by the Spirit
are children of God.
>**We will live as God's children,**
>**as heirs of God's redeeming love.**
All who are heirs of God
are also heirs with Christ.
>**We will love one another as heirs with Christ,**
>**as those loved and blessed by the living God.**

Thanksgiving and Communion

Invitation to the Offering (Psalm 104)
We worship a God who is with us to the end. When God
opens her hand, we are filled with good things. When
he takes away our breath, we die and return to dust. In
the time that we have, let us share the bounty that God
has given us in the hope that all may come to know the
bounty of our God.

Offering Prayer (Romans 8)
Merciful God,
    even as we celebrate Pentecost,
        your people groan under the crushing load
            of poverty and want.
We look around the world,
    seeing children in need
        and elders struggling to remember
            the dreams of their youth.
Help us in our weakness, Holy Spirit,
    and intercede for us
        with sighs too deep for words.
May today's offering bring hope and light
    to those who remain trapped in darkness.

Sending Forth

Benediction (Acts 2, Romans 8)
In rushing wind and tongues of flame,
go forth in the power of the living God.
We go forth as God's children.
In courage found and strength renewed,

go forth in the power of the eternal Christ.
We go forth as heirs with Christ.
In visions born, in dreams restored,
go forth in the power of the Holy Spirit.
We go forth as new creations in God's Spirit.

May 31, 2015

Trinity Sunday
Laura Jaquith Bartlett

Color

White

Scripture Readings

Isaiah 6:1-8; Psalm 29; Romans 8:12-17; John 3:1-17

Theme Ideas

Trinity Sunday is a day we celebrate the power and majesty of the Lord God, made intimate and incarnate through God's own Son, as revealed to us through the witness of the Holy Spirit. I love the triple punch of the Trinity! In the diversity of the Three-in-One, we have multiple lenses through which each of us can see the divine and hear the voice of God calling us. The most amazing miracle of the Trinity is that even in the face of our overwhelming inadequacies, each of us is called by God, loved by Christ, and equipped by the Spirit. What else can we do but respond, "I'm here; send me!"

Invitation and Gathering

Contemporary Gathering Words (Psalm 29)

(Looking up, with hands extended upward)
Greetings, divine beings!
Give glory and power to the Lord!
Let heaven bow down
to the Lord's holy splendor.
(Looking out, with hands extended toward the people)
Greetings, human beings!
Give glory and power to the Lord!
Let earth bow down
to the Lord's holy splendor.
The Lord will give strength to God's people.
The Lord will bless God's people with peace!

Call to Worship (Psalm 29, Romans 8)

The voice of God created the universe.
The voice of God calls us to worship, and we cry:
Glory!
The voice of Christ names us as sisters and brothers.
The voice of Christ calls us to worship, and we cry:
Glory! Glory!
The voice of the Spirit claims us as children of God.
The voice of the Spirit calls us to worship, and we cry:
Glory! Glory! Glory!

Opening Prayer (Isaiah 6, Romans 8, John 3)

Holy and awesome God,
you are too amazing for us to comprehend!
We thank you for the majesty, the power,
and the glory of your divine presence.
We are grateful that you came to us

in the person of a tiny, human baby.
You sent your own Son
   to enter fully into our lives.
Our connection with Christ continues
   through the power of your Holy Spirit—
      the life-giving Spirit that transforms us
         into brothers and sisters of Christ,
            full partners in the glory
               of your divine love.
With hearts overflowing, we thank you! Amen and amen.

Proclamation and Response

Prayer of Confession (Isaiah 6, Romans 8, John 3)
God, you come to us in a blaze of glory,
   but feeling unworthy of your presence,
      we cower and hide.
You invite us to become one with Christ,
   but in our fear of the demand to take up our cross,
      we pull back from you.
You offer us the gift of new life,
   but we roll our eyes,
      convinced of our knowledge of human biology
         and the impossibility of resurrection.
You manifest yourself to us in so many ways,
   but we have become experts at dodging, avoiding,
      and rationalizing our refusal to follow your ways.
Forgive us, Holy One.
Come to us once again, we pray.
Open our eyes to your glory.
Open our hearts to your love.
Open our minds to your divine presence in our lives.
Amen.

Words of Assurance (Romans 8, John 3)
God's own child was born on earth, in our midst,
as a sign of God's deep and abiding love
for each one of us.
Through the witness of the Holy Spirit,
we claim this love for our own.
We are the forgiven and loved children of God!

Passing the Peace of Christ (Trinity Sunday)
(As you move through the room to greet one another, use one of these spoken greetings as we celebrate the community of the Holy Trinity.)
May the love of God be with you.
May the peace of Christ be with you.
May the power of the Holy Spirit be with you.

Prayer of Preparation (Isaiah 6, Romans 8, John 3)
Mighty God, may we come to know your glory,
as we listen to your holy word.
Loving Christ, may we be born again with you,
as we listen to your holy word.
Living Spirit, may we claim our inheritance
as children of God,
as we listen to your holy word.
Three-in-One, transform us by your word this day.
Amen.

Response to the Word (Isaiah 6, Romans 8, John 3)
When we are dazzled by your glory, O God,
prompt us to answer your call:
I'm here; send me.
When we are confused by theological arguments,
prompt us to answer your call:
I'm here; send me.

When we are sure we don't have what we need,
prompt us to answer your call:
>**I'm here; send me.**
When we forget our call to serve your children,
prompt us to answer your call:
>**I'm here; send me.**
God, you equip us, inspire us, and love us.
We answer you now:
>**I'm here; send me.**

Thanksgiving and Communion

Offering Prayer (Isaiah 6, Romans 8)
Dear God, your scriptures paint a majestic picture
>of your holy temple.
But instead of commanding us
>to cower before your might,
>>you call us to join with you
>>>in building your reign here on earth.
May these gifts become tangible evidence
>of our commitment to answer your call. Amen.

Sending Forth

Benediction (Isaiah 6, Romans 8, John 3)

One:	We have experienced the glory and majesty of God.
Two:	*Now go forth to roll up your sleeves and work for justice.*
All:	**We have been born again in the love of Christ Jesus who offers us nothing less than eternal life.**

One: Now go forth to offer hope to those
         for whom hope has died.
All: **We have been transformed by the witness
         of the Holy Spirit.**
Two: *Go forth to testify to the resilience of love.*
All: **We go in peace to serve God and your
         neighbor. Amen.**

June 7, 2015

Second Sunday after Pentecost, Proper 5
B. J. Beu

[Copyright © 2014 by B. J. Beu. Used by permission.]

Color

Green

Scripture Readings

1 Samuel 8:4-20 (11:14-15); Psalm 138; 2 Corinthians 4:13–5:1; Mark 3:20-35

Theme Ideas

While Samuel was only a boy, the word of the Lord came to him saying that God had rejected the house of Eli because Eli's sons blasphemed against the Lord. In today's reading, the elders of Israel ask Samuel to appoint a king to govern them since Samuel is old and his own sons do not follow the ways of the Lord. If God was angry with Eli and his family, it was nothing to how God felt about the children of Israel wishing to be ruled by a king like other nations. How do we build something that will endure? Do we put our trust in human families, in human ingenuity and cleverness, or do we put our faith in God? The children of Israel want to have a king rule them like the other nations, but God yearns to be their only ruler and king. Jesus' mother and siblings see his ministry spinning out of control and seek to rein Jesus back in, to protect him within the family, but Jesus has a larger vision, and baldly states that biology does not define family—family are all those who do the will of God. Paul reminds the church in Corinth that while our earthly bodies age and decline, our spiritual temple is being renewed daily and will last into eternity. God calls us to build things that truly last, to look beyond simple biology to find our true family, and to look beyond the outward nature of things to see God's renewal of our inner nature.

Invitation and Gathering

Contemporary Gathering Words (1 Samuel 8, Mark 3)
Come! Here you will find a family of faith
    where you will always belong.
Come! Here you will find friends who will love you
    as a child of God.
Come! Here you will worship a King
    who rules with equity.
Whoever you are, and wherever you are
    on life's journey, you are welcome here.

Call to Worship (Mark 3)
All who need a place to belong...
    Come join the family of God.
All who seek spiritual brothers and sisters...
    Come join the family of God.
All who strive to grow in faith and love...
    Come join the family of God.

All who are unsure and feel unworthy...
Come join the family of God.

Opening Prayer (1 Samuel 8, 2 Corinthians 4, Mark 3)
Loving Mother, Caring Father,
    in the midst of our brokenness,
        knit us together as your family.
Heal our wounded hearts,
    that we may welcome the strangers into our midst
        and treat them as beloved sisters and brothers.
Swing wide the doors of our church,
    that all who seek a temple of faith
        may find in these walls
            a place where God's will is done
                and holy relationships are nurtured.
In Christ's name, we pray. Amen.

Proclamation and Response

Prayer of Confession (1 Samuel 8, Psalm 138, Mark 3)
Sovereign God,
    we so often lose our way.
You seek to be our King—
    to lead us on right paths;
    to teach us the ways of truth and life;
    to shelter us from our foes,
        yet we look to the rulers of this earth
            for leadership, wisdom, and strength.
You seek to be our comforter—
    to love us as our Father;
    to nurture us as our Mother;
    to shelter us as our Brother;
    to assure us as our Sister,

yet we look elsewhere for love,
compassion, and hope.
When our government fails us,
and our families disappoint us,
you alone remain faithful and true.
Open your arms to us once more, O God.
We will be your people,
and you will be our God and King.

Words of Assurance (Mark 3)

Christ looks to each of us and says:
"Here are my mother and my brothers.
Here are my father and my sisters.
Whoever does the will of God
is my brother, sister, mother, father."
As the family of God, as brothers and sisters of Christ,
we are loved and forgiven by our gracious God.

Passing the Peace of Christ (Mark 3)

As the family of God, let us share signs of familial love
and compassion, acceptance and forgiveness, as we pass
the peace of Christ.

Introduction to the Word (1 Corinthians 4)

Just as we have the same spirit of faith that is found in
Scripture, "I believed, and so I spoke," as we believe, so
may we speak. As the words of our faith are spoken this
day, listen for the word of God.

Response to the Word (Psalm 138, 1 Corinthians 4-5, Mark 3)

Even when our lives seem to be wasting away,
take heart.
God is renewing our inner nature day by day.
Even when leaders fail us, and our families forsake us,
take heart.

God is leading us into a family of faith.
Even when our institutions crumble,
and our schedules leave us no time for rest,
take heart.
God is offering us grace and mercy.

Thanksgiving and Communion

Invitation to the Offering (Psalm 138, Mark 3)
Give thanks and praise to the Lord with all your heart, for
God regards the lowly but perceives the haughty from far
away. As brothers and sisters of Christ, let us joyfully give
from our bounty, that all of God's family may find solace
and hope through the blessings we share this day.

Offering Prayer (1 Samuel 8, Psalm 138, Mark 3)
Holy Sovereign,
    you are our King;
        we are your people.
Forsaking the ways of the haughty,
    we reach for our brothers and sisters in faith,
        our mothers and fathers in Spirit,
            that we may care for the meek and the lowly.
Use these offerings to fulfill your will in our world,
    that all may be drawn into your family of faith
Amen.

Sending Forth

Benediction (2 Corinthians 4, Mark 3)
With God as our King,
    we go forth to build God's kingdom.

With our inner nature renewed,
we go forth to proclaim God's glory.
With our sisters and brothers in Christ,
our mothers and fathers in the faith,
We go forth to be Christ's family.
Go with God.

June 14, 2015

Third Sunday after Pentecost, Proper 6
Deborah Sokolove

Color

Green

Scripture Readings

1 Samuel 15:34–16:13; Psalm 20; 2 Corinthians 5:6-10 (11-13), 14-17; Mark 4:26-34

Theme Ideas

God does not see as humans see, but rather looks at the human heart. Dying and rising with Christ, we are made new to walk in faith, bearing the good news of God's love and grace.

Invitation and Gathering

Contemporary Gathering Words (2 Corinthians 5)
If anyone is in Christ, there is a new creation.
Come and see with the eyes of faith.
Look, everything has become new!

Call to Worship (2 Corinthians 5, Mark 4)
Come and live in God's new creation.

Everything old has passed away.
Come and rejoice in the presence of God.
The realm of God grows
like grain from the earth.
Come and see with the eyes of faith.
See, everything has become new!

Opening Prayer (2 Corinthians 5, Mark 4)
God of new beginnings,
> you make the world new each morning:
>> delighting our eyes with the tender, green shoots
>>> of early summer;
>> awakening our ears with the sounds of day.
You remind us that seeds sprout and grow
> according to your will,
>> even when we are not paying attention.
You call us to trust your love
> and remember that we are in Christ,
>> who died that we might live.
Teach us to see with the eyes of faith:
> to look beyond appearances;
> to know ourselves as your new creation,
>> members of the body of Christ,
>>> living for the sake of a broken world. Amen.

Proclamation and Response

Prayer of Confession (1 Samuel 15, Psalm 20, 2 Corinthians 5, Mark 4)
God of love and compassion,
> we take pride in our own power,
>> rather than in your holy name.
> **We have focused on our outward appearances,**

wanting people to think well of us.
We have forgotten that you alone
    can make seeds sprout and grow.
We have lived selfishly,
    thinking only of our own needs and desires.
We have not walked by faith.
Forgive us, Holy One,
    when we live as if we had not been made new
        by the power of your Spirit.

Words of Assurance (Psalm 20, 2 Corinthians 5)
The Holy One, who makes all things new,
    surrounds us with love and grace.
In the name of Christ, you are forgiven.
In the name of Christ, you are forgiven.
Glory to God.

Passing the Peace of Christ (1 Samuel 15, Psalm 20, 2 Cor-
inthians 5, Mark 4)
Christ died for all, so that we might live for one another.
In gratitude for this great gift, let us greet one another
with signs of peace.
The peace of Christ be with you.
The peace of Christ be with you always.

Introduction to the Word (Mark 4)
Jesus spoke in parables, yet many were able to hear his
message. May God open our ears and our hearts to receive the word this day. Amen.

Response to the Word (2 Corinthians 5, Mark 4)
The realm of God is all around us. Look and see with the
eyes of faith.

Thanksgiving and Communion

Invitation to the Offering (Mark 4)

In gratitude for the abundance of God's grace, let us bring our gifts and offerings.

Offering Prayer (Mark 4)

God of seed and harvest, God of grain and mustard seed,
God of roots and branches,
use our gifts as seeds for the coming harvest—
a harvest of love throughout your realm.
Amen.

Great Thanksgiving

Christ be with you.
And also with you.
Lift up your hearts.
We lift them up to God.
Let us give our thanks to the Holy One.
It is right to give our thanks and praise.

It is a right, good, and a joyful thing
always and everywhere to give our thanks to you.
You led Samuel to anoint David, Jesse's son,
when Saul was no longer able to be king.
You cause seeds to grow into heavy heads full of grain;
and make everything new in the love of Christ.
And so, with your creatures on earth
and all the heavenly chorus,
we praise your name and join their unending hymn:
**Holy, holy, holy Lord, God of power and might,
heaven and earth are full of your glory.**

**Hosanna in the highest. Blessed is the one
who comes in the name of the Lord.
Hosanna in the highest.**

Holy are you, and holy is your child, Jesus Christ,
who taught his disciples in stories and parables
that the realm of God is all around us
when we look with the eyes of faith.

On the night in which he gave himself up,
Jesus took bread, gave thanks to you,
broke the bread, and gave it to the disciples, saying:
"Take, eat; this is my body which is given for you.
Do this in remembrance of me."
When the supper was over, Jesus took the cup,
offered thanks and gave it to the disciples, saying:
"Drink from this, all of you;
this is my life in the new covenant,
poured out for you and for many,
for the forgiveness of sins.
Do this, as often as you drink it,
in remembrance of me."
And so, in remembrance of your mighty acts
in Jesus Christ, we proclaim the mystery of faith.
Christ has died.
Christ is risen.
Christ will come again.
Pour out your Holy Spirit on us,
and on these gifts of bread and wine.
Make them be for us the body and blood of Christ,
that we may be the body of Christ
to a world that yearns to be made new.

Maker of seed and harvest, Spirit of story and parable,
Giver of new life,
we praise your holy, eternal, loving name. Amen.

Sending Forth

Benediction (2 Corinthians 5)
Go into the world as a new creation in Christ.
In the power of the Holy Spirit,
bear the good news of God's love and grace.

June 21, 2015

Fourth Sunday after Pentecost,
Proper 7/Father's Day

B. J. Beu

[Copyright © 2014 by B. J. Beu. Used by permission.]

Color

Green

Scripture Readings

1 Samuel 17:(1a, 4-11, 19-23), 32-49; Psalm 9:9-20;
2 Corinthians 6:1-13; Mark 4:35-41

Theme Ideas

God is on the side of the oppressed and defenseless, defending the powerless and lifting up the downtrodden. While the Hebrew Scriptures portray God's vindication through earthly violence and military might, the epistle speaks of overcoming evil through weapons of righteousness. The Gospel depicts the one who carried no sword as having power over the very elements of earth and water. God's presence in our lives gives us the courage to face danger and overcome our fears, for God listens and responds to those who call on the name of the Lord.

Invitation and Gathering

Contemporary Gathering Words (Mark 4)

Where can we turn when storms threaten?
In Christ's love, we rest in peace.
Where do we look when waves crash?
In Christ's bosom, we fear no evil.
What do we listen for when thunder booms?
In Christ's call, we find our strength.
Come, take the hand of the one who stills the waters.

Call to Worship (Mark 4)

Dangers are all around us.
Call on the Lord and find safety.
Fears and doubt overwhelm us.
Call on the Lord and find faith.
Waves of despair wash over us.
Call on the Lord and find peace.

Opening Prayer (Psalm 9, Mark 4)

Lord of wind and sea,
when the storms of life
threaten to overwhelm us,
you speak a word of peace
and calm the raging waters;
when the gales and tempests
threaten to sweep us away,
you rebuke the winds
and still the roiling seas.
You are our stronghold in times of trouble.
You silence the fears within our troubled hearts
and fill us with wonder at your awesome power,
that we may search inward, find our quiet center,
and meet you there. Amen.

Proclamation and Response

Prayer of Confession (1 Samuel 17, 2 Corinthians 2, Mark 4)
> God of power and might,
>> our fears are greater than our foes.
> Every adversary seems like the warrior Goliath.
> Every tool at our disposal
>> seems like a harmless slingshot.
> Teach us your lessons once more:
>> that the weapons of violence and hate
>>> are no match for the tools of righteousness;
>> that purity, knowledge, patience,
>>> kindness, and genuine love,
>>>> are stronger than any force
>>>>> that is set against us.
> This we pray in the name of the one
>> who overcame violence by turning the other cheek,
>> and who calmed the raging waters
>>> with a single word: "Peace!" Amen.

Words of Assurance (Mark 4)
> The one whose hand stills the waters reaches out to us
>> to share God's forgiveness and peace.
> Be at peace, for all is well.

Passing the Peace of Christ (Mark 4)
> With a single word, "Peace," Jesus calmed the stormy seas and silenced the howling winds. With a single word Jesus invites us into a mystery deeper than our reason can comprehend. In the mystery of God, let us share the awesome power of the peace of Christ.

Introduction to the Word (2 Corinthians 6:2)
> Now is the acceptable time. Now is the day of salvation.

Listen well to the words of life spoken this day. Listen and you will live.

Response to the Word or Benediction (2 Corinthians 6:4-7)
Do not accept the grace of God in vain. But as servants of God, let us commend ourselves through purity, knowledge, patience, kindness, holiness of spirit, genuine love, truthful speech, and the power of God.

Thanksgiving and Communion

Invitation to the Offering (1 Samuel 17, Psalm 9)
God watches over us as a shepherd watches over her flock. Christ cares for us, and saves us, from those who would do us harm. Let us offer our thanks and gratitude as we share your gifts with a weak and weary world.

Offering Prayer (Psalm 9, 2 Corinthians 6)
Gracious God,
  you promise to be a stronghold for the oppressed,
    a stronghold in times of trouble for those in need.
May the gifts we bring this day
  truly be a source of strength for the oppressed
    and a source of rejoicing for those in need.
Let us give out of our abundance,
  for whether we are rich or poor,
    in you we possess everything. Amen.

Sending Forth

Benediction (Psalm 9, Mark 4)
Even amidst the storms of life,
  God gives us the strength and courage

to brave the waves, ride out the squalls,
and face the future unafraid.
Even amidst the ravages of this world,
God is our stronghold,
the One who brings us peace.

June 28, 2015

Fifth Sunday after Pentecost, Proper 8
Mary J. Scifres

[Copyright © 2014 by Mary J. Scifres. Used by permission.]

Color

Green

Scripture Readings

2 Samuel 1:1, 17-27; Psalm 130; 2 Corinthians 8:7-15; Mark 5:21-43

Theme Ideas

Even in these disparate scriptures, a theme of hope emerges. In the midst of her despair, hope gives courage to a hemorrhaging woman to touch Jesus' garment and be healed. In the face of death, hope gives a synagogue leader faith that Jesus can heal his child. In a troubled and troubling community, hope causes Paul to call the Corinthian leaders to stewardship and generosity. Even in the midst of grief, hope inspires David to write a poignant song of lament and praise for his beloved friends who have died. Even the psalmist, crying out from the depths, calls us to wait for God, hoping and trusting in God's steadfast love. Hope in the midst of despair is a powerful gift, a challenging call, and a healing balm.

Invitation and Gathering

Contemporary Gathering Words (Psalm 130)
As we gather and worship this day,
we wait with faith and hope.
As we reflect on a troubled world,
we wait with faith and hope.
As we face the sadness and sorrow of life,
we wait with faith and hope.
As we celebrate the joys and gifts that abound,
we wait with faith and hope.
Come! Let us worship with faith and hope this day.

Call to Worship (Psalm 130, Mark 5)
Wait for the Lord. Wait with faith and hope.
We come as a people of faith,
yearning to touch the hem of hope.
Wait for Christ's healing and strength.
We come as a people strengthened by God,
yearning to touch the hem of healing.
Waiting and hoping, we come to worship.
We come to be healed.

Opening Prayer (Psalm 130, Mark 5)
Healing and Healer God,
call us to rise in faith this day.
Strengthen us to walk into the light
of your healing and your hope.
Inspire us to trust your promises,
and celebrate the power of your steadfast love.
In the healing name of Christ, we pray. Amen.

Proclamation and Response

Prayer of Confession (Psalm 130, Mark 5)
> Out of our deepest need,
>> we cry to you, O God.
> Listen to our voices:
>> Have mercy on us.
>> Have mercy on us.
>> Have mercy on us.
> *(Silent prayer may follow.)*
> Heal us, Merciful God,
>> that we might receive your forgiveness
>>> and find balm for our sorrows.
> In Christ's gracious name, we pray. Amen.

Words of Assurance (Psalm 130)
> God does not hold our sins against us.
> Receive the gift of grace,
>> for we are forgiven and loved by God!

Passing the Peace of Christ (2 Samuel, 2 Corinthians 8)
> Friends, we are surrounded by our beloved sisters
> and brothers in this community of faith. Share signs of
> hope, love, and faith, as you pass the peace of Christ
> this day.

Prayer of Preparation (Psalm 130)
> We wait, O God.
> Our souls wait and hope
>> for your guiding presence this day.
> Speak to us now,
>> that we may hear your voice
>>> and know your truth.

Response to the Word (Psalm 130, 2 Corinthians 8, Mark 5)
We have waited and listened. Now let us commit ourselves to being the church and doing the work that God
has created us to do.
God of strength and hope,
inspire us to reach out for your healing touch,
that we may walk forth in faith.
strengthen us to fulfill our commitments
and our calling.
With eagerness and joy,
In hope and trust, we pray. Amen.

Prayer of Preparation (Psalm 130)
(Use to lead into a Service of Healing.)
We wait, O God.
Our souls wait and hope
for your healing presence this day.
Touch us now,
that we may know your healing balm
and your steadfast love.

Response to the Word—A Litany of Healing (2 Samuel 1, Psalm 130)
We, who once felt mighty, feel fallen and grieved.
Strengthen us, Healer God,
that we may know again
the joy of childish confidence.
We, who once felt whole, feel hurt and broken.
Mend us, Healer God,
that we may know health and wholeness
once more. Amen.

Thanksgiving and Communion

Invitation to the Offering (2 Corinthians 8)
>God calls us to give generously, even sacrificially. Why? Not because God wants others to have financial ease while we have financial difficulties, but because God wants balance and equity. If our surplus can fill someone's deficit, let us give it all. For those among us whose storehouses are empty, may our gifts provide the surplus they need to find hope in the midst of despair.

Offering Prayer (2 Corinthians 8, Mark 5)
>Gather these gifts and strengthen our generosity,
>>that none may have too much
>>>and none may have too little.
>
>Bless these gifts and strengthen our ministry,
>>that all may know your healing balm
>>>and your promise of hope. Amen.

Sending Forth

Benediction (Psalm 130, Mark 5)
>Get up and go!
>>**We have been healed to go forth in the world.**
>
>Get up and go!
>>**We have been strengthened to go forth with hope.**
>
>Get up and go!
>>**We are ready; we are going!**

July 5, 2015

Sixth Sunday after Pentecost, Proper 9
Rebecca J. Kruger Gaudino

Color

Green

Scripture Readings

2 Samuel 5:1-5, 9-10; Psalm 48; 2 Corinthians 12:2-10; Mark 6:1-13

Theme Ideas

Today we read the stories of two young men, both of them about thirty years old, both powerful, both loved by God: David and Jesus. In David, we find someone very sure of himself, quick to use power in ways that make us at times uncomfortable. Note that while Jerusalem becomes known as "the city of David" (2 Samuel 5:9), the psalmist correctly calls it "the city belonging to our God" (Psalm 48:1). How different is the other young man, Jesus: whose power is so easily dismissed and disregarded, who sends out, not armies, but disciples two by two with nothing but a staff and the clothes on their backs. And yet this young man and his disciples changed lives in amazing ways. In Jesus, Christians are given another model of power: a "power...made perfect in weakness" (2 Corinthians 12:9).

Invitation and Gathering

Contemporary Gathering Words (Psalm 48, NRSV and CEB)
(Project the following words on a screen along with pictures of the towers, citadels, and ramparts of Old Jerusalem. Also include drawings of the temple of Solomon. Look for representations that convey the glory and might described by Psalm 48.)
Imagine ancient Jerusalem, set on God's holy mountain.
Count its towers, and walk through its citadels!
See its soaring defenses!
Surely God is great and worthy of praise!
Imagine the temple of Solomon, God's holy house.
Enter its beautiful gates!
Stand in its courts!
Think of God's great, faithful love!
Tell your children about this mighty God
of unwavering love.
This is God, our God, the One who will lead us,
even to the very end!
This is God, our God, forever and always!

Call to Worship (Psalm 48)
Our God is great and worthy of praise!
God's holy mountain is beautiful.
It is the joy of the whole world!
In the midst of your temple, O God,
we dwell in your faithful love!
Your praise and reputation, O God,
go far beyond this mountain
to the far corners of the earth!

Let us walk about this holy mountain,
and behold its towers and fortifications.
Then let us teach our children
about our strong and righteous God.
>**God is the One who will lead us,**
>**even to the very end!**
>**This is God, our God, forever and always!**

Opening Prayer (2 Samuel 5, Psalm 48, Mark 6, 2 Corinthians 12)
>We gather in your presence, God of holiness and power,
>>to praise you for your wisdom, justice, and might,
>>>on which our world is founded.
>Your power endures forever, Sovereign God!
>The magnificent spinning of the planets
>>and the mysterious rise and fall
>>>of rulers and nations fill us with awe.
>We see the manifestation of your power,
>>even in the aching, fragile places of our lives.
>We have come to meditate on your faithful love—
>>a love that moves in might and in vulnerability.
>In the name of Jesus, giver of grace, we pray. Amen.

Proclamation and Response

Prayer of Confession (2 Samuel 5, Psalm 48, Mark 6, 2 Corinthians 12)
>Jesus Christ, child of God,
>>we would rather know you as victorious
>>>and worship you as all-powerful,
>>>>than see you as a vulnerable human being,
>>>>>insulted and rejected by others.
>We prefer strength and victory in our lives

over weakness and failure.
Forgive us when we turn away
from pain and humiliation,
and do not look for your grace and power
in servanthood and weakness.
In all the happenings of our lives,
may your grace be sufficient for our needs. Amen.

Words of Assurance (Psalm 48, 2 Corinthians 12)
The grace of Jesus Christ is sufficient for us all.
We are forgiven and made strong in our weakness.
Great is God and worthy of our praise!

Passing the Peace of Christ (Mark 6)
We welcome all who enter this house today, for all are
called by Jesus Christ.
May the grace and peace of Christ be with you.
And also with you.

Introduction to the Word (Psalm 48, Mark 6)
Let us listen with open hearts and minds for God's wisdom and guidance.

Response to the Word (Psalm 48, Mark 6)
O God, you lead us throughout our lives.
We welcome your word and listen for your wisdom.
We honor you as you teach us today. Amen.

Thanksgiving and Communion

Offering Prayer (Psalm 48, Mark 6)
Jesus Christ,
you teach us to look for your presence and power
in the midst of vulnerability and need.

May those who receive the gifts we have given
    experience your power in new and amazing ways.
May your power rest upon them,
    lift them up, heal them,
        and draw them near to you.
In the name of the one who shared his very life. Amen.

Invitation to Communion (Mark 6)
    Jesus sent out his disciples two by two with nothing but
their staffs and the clothes on their backs. Wherever they
went, they must have arrived hungry and tired, needing
food and shelter. In the spirit of the one who sends us
out, we welcome all who have traveled here today. In
different ways we are all hungry, we all need shelter, we
all require a place of caring and acceptance. Draw near
to this table under the sheltering roof of this house. Prepare for this meal—a meal that will strengthen us with
the presence and power of Jesus Christ. Welcome to this
home and table, brothers and sisters all!

Sending Forth

Benediction (Psalm 48, 2 Corinthians 12)
    Even in our weakness and failure,
    the grace of Jesus Christ will see us through!
        We go forth with hope in God's faithful love,
        knowing that the grace of Jesus Christ
        will see us through!

July 12, 2015

Seventh Sunday after Pentecost, Proper 10
Laura Jaquith Bartlett

Color

Green

Scripture Readings

2 Samuel 6:1-5, 12b-19; Psalm 24; Ephesians 1:3-14; Mark 6:14-29

Theme Ideas

Dancing has a long and conflicted history in the church. Many seniors in our churches remember a time when dancing was considered taboo for "good Christians." But dancing as a joyful response to God's blessings dates back to at least the time of Moses, when Miriam led worship on the shores of the Red Sea. Second Samuel relates the tale of King David dancing with abandon before the Lord. Even here, however, such unfettered exuberance and praise was met with Michal's disapproval. The Mark passage, meanwhile, shows us that dancing (like any other activity) can be twisted and exploited when it is not an act of worship. The Ephesians reading is full of the Good News of God's love for us in Jesus Christ. Together with David and Miriam and a whole host of others, let us dance for joy in response to God's abundant blessings!

Invitation and Gathering

Contemporary Gathering Words (2 Samuel 6, Psalm 24)
All the earth belongs to God.
In the green meadows and deep forests,
let's dance before the Lord!
All the waters of the earth were created by God.
Along sandy beaches and shady riverbanks,
let's dance before the Lord!
Everything that is on the earth belongs to God.
With all our sisters and brothers,
let's dance before the Lord!
Come and join the dance as we celebrate God's love!

Call to Worship (Ephesians 1)
Bless God, the Mother and Father of our Lord
Jesus Christ.
God has blessed us abundantly in Christ.
We are claimed as God's own children
through the love of Jesus Christ.
God has blessed us abundantly in Christ.
The Holy Spirit is the down payment on our inheritance
as God's own redeemed people.
God has blessed us abundantly in Christ.
Let us worship the God of abundant blessings!

Opening Prayer (2 Samuel 6, Psalm 24, Ephesians 1)
God of the ages,
you have been present with us
since the beginning.

You have showered us throughout history
>with the blessings of your love.
In this place, at this moment,
>>we join together to praise you, to worship you,
>>>and to rejoice in your saving grace.
For bringing heaven and earth together
>>in the redemptive love of Jesus Christ,
>>we thank you.
Empower our voices to proclaim your greatness,
>>even as our feet dance the good news
>>>of your love for all the earth. Amen.

Proclamation and Response

Prayer of Confession (2 Samuel 6, Psalm 24, Ephesians 1, Mark 6)
>Dear God, you have given us good gifts
>>with which to praise you,
>>>but we have turned communal worship
>>>>into a spectator sport.
>You call us to proclaim your love
>>with every fiber of our being,
>>>but we sit glued to our pews.
>Instead of dancing our joy at being in your presence,
>>we hang back and watch the "professionals,"
>>>believing we are too old, too clumsy,
>>>>too untrained to do it properly.
>Help us remember that since the dawn of creation,
>>you have been training us for praise.
>Forgive us our arrogance and perfectionism,
>>and empower us to use our bodies

to express our joy and delight
at the vast expanse of your love.
Teach us to sing, to dance, and to join hands with others,
as we create the blessed community of grace
you envision for our world.
We pray in the name of your Incarnate Son,
Jesus Christ. Amen.

Words of Assurance (Ephesians 1)

God has already accomplished your salvation
through Christ Jesus.
This is true today and every day.
Dance in the freedom of God's forgiveness!

Passing the Peace of Christ (2 Samuel 6)

(Consider having instrumentalists play "Lord of the Dance" during the passing of the peace, and use these or similar words to introduce it.)

Our [*band/organist/pianist/guitarist*] will play "Lord of the Dance" as we pass the peace of Christ today. I invite you to use the music to put a bit of a bounce in your step or in your voice as you exchange holy greetings with one another. Let's celebrate the love of God that we have found here in Christ's community.

Response to the Word (2 Samuel 6, Ephesians 1)

(Have the musicians again play the music for "Lord of the Dance" as the preacher or liturgist prays these words.)

Lord of the Dance,
we thank you for calling us
into the good news of your community.
Your amazing love makes us your children—
sisters and brothers of Jesus—
and makes us as full participants

in Christ's salvation.
Your Holy Spirit delivers our inheritance:
    our sacred identity as your own people.
Let us now join you in the dance of celebration,
    as we proclaim your love for the world.
(Musicians lead the refrain of the "Lord of the Dance.")

Thanksgiving and Communion

Offering Prayer (Ephesians 1)
Generous God, may our very lives
    be a thanksgiving offered to you.
You created the earth in all its richness and blessing.
Help us remember that it all belongs to you.
Take these offerings and use them for your glory.
Take our lives, and use us,
    always and everywhere, for your glory.
In Christ's name, we pray. Amen.

Sending Forth

Benediction (2 Samuel 6, Ephesians 1)
Go dancing into the world today
    as a blessing from our creator God.
Go dancing into the world today
    as you share your inheritance in Christ's salvation.
Go dancing into the world today
    as an affirmation of the promise of the Holy Spirit.
Go dancing into the world today
    as you serve others and proclaim the good news
    of God's abundant peace and love. Amen.

July 19, 2015

Eighth Sunday after Pentecost, Proper 11
B. J. Beu

Color

Green

Scripture Readings

2 Samuel 7:1-14a; Psalm 89:20-37; Ephesians 2:11-22; Mark 6:30-34, 53-56

Theme Ideas

God is always working to bring us peace. After defeating Israel's enemies, David is intent upon building God a house, but God wishes only for David to continue his role as a shepherd—now as prince over Israel—that the people may know the blessings of peace. True kingship and lineage come through shepherding love and by bringing enemies together in friendship and kinship, not by keeping them as vassals under foot. The peace Jesus brought, the peace attested to in both Mark and Ephesians, is not accomplished by force of arms or family lineage, but through sacrificial love—the love of a shepherd, the love that brings reconciliation of enemies into a new and holy people. Ultimately, the peace that David brought through force of arms could not stand—despite God's assurances that David's line would last forever. Perhaps God realized that the peace Israel hoped for by vanquishing its enemies was no real peace.

Invitation and Gathering

Contemporary Gathering Words (Ephesians 2, Mark 6)
Overwhelmed and alone,
> **the Lord is our shepherd.**
In sickness unto death,
> **Christ restores our life.**
At war with one another,
> **the Spirit makes us one.**
Let us worship God,
the One who brings us peace.

Call to Worship (Ephesians 2, Mark 6)
Are you weary from your labors?
> **Here you will find rest.**
Are you divided from family and friends?
> **Here you will find peace.**
Are you spent from your efforts to bring God's kingdom?
> **Here you will find strength.**
Are you looking for a shepherd to watch over you?
> **Here you will find the one who makes us whole.**

Opening Prayer (Psalm 89, Ephesians 2, Mark 6)
Rock of our salvation,
> like a river in the desert,
> > your love quenches our thirst for righteousness;

like the bounty of the sea,
    your covenant feeds our hunger for peace.
Your ways are like the moon,
    an enduring witness in the sky
        to the eternal nature of your love and care.
Be present in our worship, Lord,
    and heal the wounds that divide us,
        for we long to be fashioned into a new humanity,
            and to be joined together into a holy temple,
                through Christ our shepherd. Amen.

Proclamation and Response

Prayer of Confession (Ephesians 2, Mark 6)
Shepherding God,
    we need your Spirit to guide us;
    we need your peace to help us set aside
        the things that divide us.
Forgive us when we cling to our grievances,
    and dismiss our adversaries as strangers and aliens
        unworthy of your love.
You seek to heal our vision,
    that we may see all people
        as members of your household.
Forgive us when we refuse to be built
    into a spiritual temple
        with Christ as the cornerstone,
            if it means opening our hearts
                to those who have wronged us.
Heal the hardness of our hearts,
    that we may embrace your shepherding love.
    Amen.

Words of Assurance (Ephesians 2)
As members of the household of God,
Christ brings us together as a holy temple,
a dwelling place for the Lord of hosts.
In Christ, we are healed and become a new humanity,
loved and forgiven by the Lord of life.

Passing the Peace of Christ (Ephesians 2)
Christ's love breaks down the walls that divide us. In joy and celebration of this great gift, let us turn to one another and share signs of the peace that makes us one.

Introduction to the Word (2 Samuel 7)
The One who traveled with the Hebrew people in the Ark of the Covenant is with us still. The One who remains faithful continues to speak to those whose minds are open and whose hearts are receptive. Listen for the word of God.

Response to the Word (2 Samuel 7, Psalm 89)
Like the moon in the sky, God's word endures forever. If we hear God's words and allow ourselves to be knit together as one, we will be built into a spiritual dwelling place for God.

Thanksgiving and Communion

Invitation to the Offering (2 Samuel 7, Ephesians 2)
As disparate peoples from many lands, we have been knit together by God into a holy community. From strangers, Christ has built us together into a holy temple in the Lord. With thankful hearts to the One who continues to bless us, let us be generous as we collect today's offering.

Offering Prayer (2 Samuel 7, Ephesians 2, Mark 6)
    Bringer of peace,
        you shaped your people
            and gave them a home;
        you gave David rest from the wars
            assailing your people.
    We thank and praise you this day,
        for calling us to feed in your pastures
            and rest safely in your fields.
    In our gratitude for your steadfast love,
        receive the gifts we bring this day,
            that they may be signs of our love
                for the one you sent
                    to be our shepherd. Amen.

Sending Forth

Benediction (Psalm 89, Ephesians 2)
    The old hatreds have been swallowed up.
        In Christ we know love.
    The old arguments taste bitter in our mouths.
        In Christ we have peace.
    The old wounds have been anointed with holy oil.
        In Christ we find healing.
    The old walls have come crumbling down.
        In Christ we are one.

July 26, 2015

Ninth Sunday after Pentecost, Proper 12
Mary J. Scifres

Color

Green

Scripture Readings

2 Samuel 11:1-15; Psalm 14; Ephesians 3:14-21; John 6:1-21

Theme Ideas

Today's theme emerges from the Ephesians reading: Rooted and grounded in love, we grow in faith and discipleship. This is a prayer for the church at Ephesus, but this same prayer can be made for any congregation throughout Christendom. Even when we use other scriptures today, the strong root of love can be a powerful image, and this scripture can serve as a psalm or doxology. A foundation of love could have stopped David's sinful decision to take another's wife and then arrange for the murder of her husband. The root of love led Jesus to feed thousands, miraculously and abundantly. This strong root of love is the foundation that can strengthen any follower of God to grow in spirit and faith.

Invitation and Gathering

Contemporary Gathering Words (Ephesians 3, John 6)

From a strong root of love, anything is possible.
Because of love, Jesus taught and preached,
    healed and fed, lived and died.
Out of love, churches have been born,
    Christianity has grown,
    and God's word has spread.
Because of love, we are connected to others,
    we create families and friendships,
    we find community.
Out of love, we grow as disciples,
    we grow in mercy and grace,
    we grow with love as the foundation
    and center of our lives.
Perhaps the Beatles were right: All we need is love.

Call to Worship (Ephesians 3)

Come, sisters and brothers, rejoice in God's glory.
We give praise for God's endless love!
Come, sisters and brothers, sing of God's riches.
We are blessed with the gift of God's love.
Come, sisters and brothers, celebrate the Spirit's calling.
We give thanks for the Spirit within!

Opening Prayer (Ephesians 3)

Come and dwell in us, Christ Jesus.
Plant a seed of love in our hearts and in our lives,
    that the strong root of love may grow within us.
Transform each one of us, transform this church,
    and transform the world,
        in faith and love, we pray. Amen.

Proclamation and Response

Prayer of Confession (Ephesians 3)

Holy Love, to you we pray.
We pray to you, O Christ,
    for you show us the way of love.
We pray to love,
    for God is love.
We pray for love,
    for love is the root of grace
        and the foundation of mercy.
Forgive us when we lose our grounding in love,
    and act in ways that separate us from you
        and from one another.
Forgive us when hatred and enmity
    take root and weaken the love
        you have planted within us.
Reclaim the foundation of our lives, Loving One,
    that we may grow in faith and strength
        from the root of love. Amen.

Words of Assurance (Ephesians 3, John 6)

May God grant you the power to grasp the fullness
    of love's width, length, height, and depth.
For God's love is big enough
    to gather the fragments of our broken lives
    and transform them into abundance.
In the name of Christ Jesus, we are forgiven.
In the love of God, we are made whole.
With the strong root of love,
    let us grow in God's glorious grace.

Passing the Peace of Christ (Ephesians 3)

With strong roots of love, let us strengthen one another
by sharing signs of peace and grace.

Introduction to the Word (Ephesians 3)

Listen and be strengthened in your inner being. Open yourselves to the presence of Christ that lives in your hearts and lives. By listening and opening yourselves to God, you will know Christ's love so deeply that its strong root will grow mighty and strong within you.

Response to the Word (Ephesians 3)

God is able to do far more than we ask.
Glory to God in the highest!
Because Christ is in our hearts,
we will be more than we ever imagined.
Glory to God in the highest!
In the power of God's Holy Spirit,
we are able to do more than we thought possible.
Glory to God in the highest!
Together, this body of Christ
can transform meager loaves and fish
into a miraculous abundance of love
for a world in need.

—Or—

Response to the Word (Ephesians 3)

In the unity of this body of Christ,
God gathers our meager loaves and fish
to create a miraculous abundance of love
for a world in need.
Glory to God in the highest!
May we trust these promises and live this truth:
The love of Christ is beyond knowledge.
It's height and depth can scarcely be grasped,
yet lives within each of us.
Glory to God in the highest!

Thanksgiving and Communion

Invitation to the Offering (Ephesians 3, John 6)

A loaf of bread here, an extra fish there, a widow's penny, a child's coin, a rich man's millions...any gift shared in love can transform the world. Let us give generously from the strong root of love.

Offering Prayer (Ephesians 3, John 6)

Bless these gifts with your love and grace.
Transform even our meager offerings and leftovers
    into abundant possibilities.
Transform us, that rooted and grounded in love,
    we may give all that we have, and all that we are,
        to serve you and your world
            with a love that knows no bounds. Amen.

Invitation to Communion (John 6)

Why have you come to this place?
    We have come to find Jesus.
Why have you come today?
    We are tired in body and spirit.
Jesus bids you sit and be at ease.
    We are hungry with nothing to eat.
Come and eat your fill.
    But there are only five barley loaves and two fish.
There is plenty for all.
    Will we find wholeness here?
Jesus gathers the fragments of our lives,
that nothing may be lost.
Come, all will be fed with God's love.
(B. J. Beu)

Communion Prayer (John 6)
>God of our hopes and dreams,
>>we are empty and long to be filled;
>>we are hungry and long to be fed;
>>we are lost and long to be found.
>God of our love,
>>and pick up the pieces of our lives,
>>>just as Jesus gathered up the fragments
>>>>of the five loaves and two fish
>>>>>after feeding the five thousand.
>By the power of your Holy Spirit,
>>bless these gifts of bread and wine,
>>>that they may become for us the bread of life,
>>>>and the cup of eternal love.
>Call us anew to eat our fill,
>>that we may find our true nourishment in Jesus,
>>>the bread of heaven. Amen.
>(B. J. Beu and Mary J. Scifres)

Response to Communion (Ephesians 3, John 6)
>Jesus feeds the multitudes.
>>**We are rooted in God's love.**
>Jesus brings us hope.
>>**We are strengthened by God's Spirit.**
>Jesus gathers the lost and the scattered.
>>**We are rooted in God's love.**
>In Jesus, we are made whole.
>(B. J. Beu)

Sending Forth

Benediction
>May you know the love of Christ.
>May you dwell in this glorious gift.
>>**From the strong root of love,**
>>**we go forth to give love to God's world!**

August 2, 2015

Tenth Sunday after Pentecost, Proper 13
Jamie Greening

Color

Green

Scripture Readings

2 Samuel 11:26–12:13a; Psalm 51:1-12; Ephesians 4:1-16; John 6:24-35

Theme Ideas

Though at first glance these readings appear disparate, the presence of God's gifts unites them. In John 6, Jesus states that it was not Moses who provided the bread from heaven, it was God. And now Jesus, as the "bread of life," is the fulfillment of God's gift of spiritual food and water. Ephesians 4 describes multiple gifts, including the gift of the church, the gift of unity, the gift of the Holy Spirit, and the gift of leadership. Together, these gifts nurture Christ's followers toward maturity. In Psalm 51, after the ugly specter of David's shameful scandal, and murder of a lover's husband, God lamented: "I would have given even more" (2 Samuel 12:8).

Invitation and Gathering

Contemporary Gathering Words (Ephesians 4)
God lives in all of us.
God works through all of us.
God provides gifts to all of us.
God gives hope to all of us.
God brings unity to all of us.
God lives in all of us.

—Or—

Contemporary Gathering Words (Ephesians 4)
The Spirit weaves us together.
Even the broken threads of our lives
    can be trimmed and melded.
Even the tattered seams
    can be mended and joined.
Diverse colors, various patterns,
    and unique fabrics...
    all are welcome here!
Bring now your gifts,
    amazing and broken.
Bring now yourselves,
    awesome and torn.
Humility and gentleness,
    patience and perseverance...
    all are a part of this place.
Make now an effort to find this new unity.
Take now a step into this body,
    bound by God's peace.
May the Spirit weave us together
    with one hope and one faith,
    bound together in unity and love.
(Mary J. Scifres)

Call to Worship *(Ephesians 4)*

We have one Lord.
> **God lives in each of us.**

We have one faith.
> **God works in each of us,**

We have one baptism.
> **God gives gifts to each of us.**

We are one body.
> **God makes us all one.**

Opening Prayer *(Ephesians 4, John 6)*

Almighty God,
> we have been drawn here by your Holy Spirit
>> to celebrate the gift of Jesus Christ.

Shape and mold us in Christ,
> that we might be "completely like him."

Speak to us this day:
> through the unifying work of worship,
>> the blessed rituals of baptism and communion,
>>> and the work of your servants, our leaders.

(Optional: mention by name the church's pastors, teachers, and missionaries.)

Reveal to us the gifts of heaven:
> Truth, love, faith, and service;
>> and save us from the false gifts of this world.

We come before you hungry for love and affirmation,
> and thirsty for compassion and justice. Amen.

Proclamation and Response

Prayer of Confession *(2 Samuel 11–12, Psalm 51, Ephesians 4, John 6)*

O Generous Giver,
> we have often rejected your gift of unity,

preferring our individual rights and privileges.
Forgive us these divisions,
    and grant us the strength to be truly one body.
Correct our wayward paths,
    when we steal the gifts belonging to others—
        gifts of joy, friendship, hope, and affirmation.
Admonish us when we act like ungrateful children,
    greedily gobbling up all the best
        while leaving none for the rest.
We have disobeyed you and have lost our way,
    yet we desire that you wipe our sins away
        and make us as happy as we were
           when we first began following you. Amen.

Words of Assurance (Psalm 51, Ephesians 4)

Because we have admitted our sins
    and acknowledged our guilt,
        Christ grants us the pure gift of forgiveness.
Let us celebrate the joyful knowledge
    that we are clean and faithful again.
    We receive this gift with grateful hearts.

Passing the Peace of Christ (Ephesians 4)

God's Spirit has united our hearts in purpose and worship. Let us now bless one another with peace, saying to one another: "Live in peace."

Consecration of Worship Leaders

Women and men have been led by God's Spirit to serve as pastors and teachers and other leaders to instruct us. These people are gifts from God to help us understand and apply the ancient teachings of our faith in our contemporary world.

Introduction to the Word (Ephesians 4, John 6)

God has gifted us with the presence of the Spirit, as we participate in the work of Christ. But God has also gifted us with the blessing of holy Scripture. The bread of life, which is Christ and God's purposes in him, is revealed through God's word. May this word teach us truth and protect us from false teachings.

Response to the Word (Ephesians 4)

We are given one Spirit.
We live as one body.
We celebrate one Lord.
We share one baptism.
We all belong to one divine family.

Thanksgiving and Communion

Offering Prayer (Psalm 51, Ephesians 4)

From on high, O Lord,
    you give us the wonderful gifts of family,
        faith, reason, the Spirit, and all of creation.
In gratitude and thanks,
    we return to you a portion of the treasure trove
        you have given us.
Bless these gifts,
    that they may accomplish your work—
        to heal, comfort, rescue, and restore. Amen.

Great Thanksgiving

The Lord be with you.
And also with you.
Lift up your hearts.
We lift them up to the Lord.

Let us give thanks to the Lord, our God.
**It is right to give the Lord our thanks and praise
for all of God's wonderful gifts.**

O Great, Triune God,
    you have given innumerable gifts
    to the human family.
You have given us life and the experience of living.
You have given us reason, logic, and a conscience.
You have given creation as a testimony to your power,
    faithfulness, and creativity.
You have given the capacity for love, self-awareness,
    and the universal spiritual urge.
You have given us purpose and work.
We join with all of creation to proclaim
    our great thanksgiving to you this day.
    The gifts of God for the people of God.
To our parents of old, the matriarchs and patriarchs
    who went before us in faith,
    you gave specific gifts at specific times.
You gave them promises, and then showed yourself
    to be powerful as you fulfilled them.
You blessed them by giving them children, heirs,
    and a land to call their own.
You gave them freedom from bondage,
    and the blessing of liberty.
You gave them hope and the prophetic word
    as a gift for those who would come after them.
You gave them community, a king,
    and the language of faith to guide them.
We thank you for the work you have done in ages past,
    and for the work and the gifts that you continue
    to bless us with.

The gifts of God for the people of God.
Through our Lord, Jesus Christ,
      you have become the ultimate gift of salvation
      and truth to men and women.
Jesus gave us the words and the bread of life
      that nourishes our spirit and our minds
      in the ways of truth.
Jesus indicted the powerful
      and offered hope to the powerless.
Jesus gave victory over death and the grave
      to all who trust him.
We celebrate the work of Jesus Christ our Lord,
      who is our greatest gift.
The gifts of God for the people of God.
Today, O Lord, you have given the church your Spirit.
The Spirit gives life to lifeless law
      and liberates the soul to thrive.
The Spirit gives leadership to the church
      by calling and empowering pastors, teachers,
      missionaries, and other leaders.
The Spirit gives illumination and understanding
      for our minds and hearts.
The Spirit gives the gift of correction
      and movement toward mature love.
The Spirit gives the gift of unity,
      by calling us as one people, one body, one baptism
      and one faith. ·
The Spirit gives insight and power to work in the world
      and to fulfill the mission of Christ Jesus.
We celebrate the work of the Holy Spirit,
      given by the Lord Jesus Christ and by God,
      our Mother and Father, to the church.
The gifts of God for the people of God.

Sending Forth

Benediction (John 6)
>God desires that you have faith in the one
>>sent into the world to bless us.
>Go forth into the world as a gift from God
>>to bless the world around you
>>with faith, peace, unity, and love.

August 9, 2015

Eleventh Sunday after Pentecost, Proper 14
B. J. Beu

[Copyright © 2014 by B. J. Beu. Used by permission.]

Color

Green

Scripture Readings

2 Samuel 18:5-9, 15, 31-33; Psalm 130; Ephesians 4:25–5:2; John 6:35, 41-51

Theme Ideas

The story of king David and his son, Absalom, reads like a Greek tragedy. After plotting and scheming to usurp his father and become the new king of Israel, Absalom is ultimately killed despite David's instructions that his life be spared. David is left to weep over the loss of his son. The psalmist cries out to the Lord, noting that if God marked iniquities, none could stand. The author of Ephesians warns us to put away falsehood and anger, which lead to sin, and to replace evil talk and slander with acts of kindness and with practices that build up, rather than tear down. When Jesus describes himself as the bread of life and his hearers respond badly, he asks them not to complain among themselves, for no one can come to him unless drawn by God. Truly, nothing good comes from jealousy or complaining, anger or resentment, plotting or scheming.

Invitation and Gathering

Contemporary Gathering Words (John 6)
Come to the bread of life.
Whoever comes to Christ will never be hungry.
Whoever believes in him will never be thirsty.
Come to the bread of life.

Call to Worship (Psalm 130)
Our souls wait for the Lord,
more than those who watch for the morning.
Here, we find refuge and strength.
Here, we find forgiveness and joy.
Come! Let us worship the One who hears our cries
and is attentive to our pleas.
Our souls wait for the Lord,
more than those who watch for the morning.

Opening Prayer (Ephesians 4, John 6)
Bread of life,
we come eager to be refreshed
in body and in spirit,
for we are hungry for the bread
that comes down from heaven.
By the presence of your Holy Spirit,
build up our community of faith,
that we may abide as beloved children
and live in love as imitators of God. Amen.

Proclamation and Response

Prayer of Confession (2 Samuel 18, Psalm 130, Ephesians 4)
> Holder of our grief,
>> out of the depths we cry to you
>>> with eyes red with tears.
>
> Amidst betrayal, we often cannot save
>> the ones we love,
>>> and we are left alone in our sorrow.
>
> In our pain, we nurture anger and resentment,
>> shutting ourselves off from paths
>>> of healing and wholeness.
>
> In our anguish, we speak words
>> that are destructive and hurtful.
>
> Dry our tears, O God,
>> and lead us anew in ways of kindness and love,
>>> mercy and compassion,
>>>> that we may truly be called
>>>>> your beloved children. Amen.

Words of Assurance (Ephesians 4)
> Beloved, be imitators of God as beloved children,
>> and live as forgiven followers of Christ.

Passing the Peace of Christ (2 Samuel 18, Ephesians 4)
> Absalom turned against his father, David, who loved him, and Absalom was killed. King David was left with nothing but his grief and bitter tears. Peace—whether for a nation, a family, or oneself—is a fragile thing, never to be taken for granted. In an effort to build one another up, rather than tear one another down, let us turn and offer signs of the peace that only Christ can bring.

Introduction to the Word (John 6:45, NRSV)
The prophets proclaim: "They shall all be taught by God." As we are taught by God this day, may we be brought to Christ. Listen for the word of God.

Response to the Word (2 Samuel 18, Ephesians 4)
Do not let the sun go down on your anger.
Resentment kills.
Jealousy chokes the soul.
Bitterness poisons the spirit.
Scheming leads to tears.
Slander breaks our fellowship.
Do not let the sun go down on your anger,
but be imitators of God, and live in love
as Christ has loved us.

Thanksgiving and Communion

Invitation to the Offering (John 6)
With hearts fed by the bread of heaven, and spirits revived by the cup of salvation, let us give from our abundance as we collect today's offering.

Offering Prayer (Ephesians 4, John 6)
Bountiful God,
we came hungry in spirit,
and you fed us with the bread of life;
we came thirsting for your grace,
and you revived us with living water.
In gratitude and thanks for your many blessings,
receive the gifts we bring this day,
that they may be for the world
signs of the bread of heaven
and the fullness of your grace. Amen.

Communion Prayer (John 6)
> Bread of life,
>> you promise that whoever comes to you
>>> will never be hungry;
>> you assure us that whoever believes in you
>>> will never be thirsty.
> Come and feed us, bread of heaven,
>> for we are hungry for your truth.
> Come and satisfy our thirst, living water,
>> for we are thirsty for your righteousness.
> Give us the bread that leads to eternal life,
>> for we are weary and long to sing your praises.
> Amen.

Sending Forth

Benediction (Ephesians 4)
> Go as God's beloved children,
>> and imitate the Holy One in all you do.
> Live in love; speak with kindness;
>> touch with gentleness;
>> walk in humbleness;
>> and build up the kingdom of God.
> In all that you say, and in all that you do,
>> live in love, as Christ has loved you.

August 16, 2015

Twelfth Sunday after Pentecost, Proper 15
Mary J. Scifres
[Copyright © 2014 by Mary J. Scifres. Used by permission.]

Color

Green

Scripture Readings

1 Kings 2:10-12; 3:3-14; Psalm 111; Ephesians 5:15-20; John 6:51-58

Theme Ideas

The love of wisdom transformed the reign of King Solomon and enriched the strength and faith of our Jewish and Christian ancestors. Discernment and understanding can transform hearts and minds in our time as well, feeding us with the bread of God's wisdom and nourishing us with the understanding of Christ's teachings. Yearn for this bread always!

Invitation and Gathering

Contemporary Gathering Words (Psalm 111, Ephesians 5)
As we gather to sing and praise,
we give thanks to God.

As we prepare to discern and understand,
we give thanks to God.
As we open ourselves to wisdom and truth,
we give thanks to God.
Let us sing songs of thanksgiving and joy!

Call to Worship (1 Kings 3, Ephesians 5)
Come, seekers of wisdom and truth,
God's wisdom has called us here.
Come, lovers of Christ's teachings and guidance,
Christ's love has called us here.
Come, singers of thanksgiving and praise,
the Spirit's presence has gathered us here!

Opening Prayer (1 Kings 3, Ephesians 5)
Wisdom from on high,
pour your Spirit upon us,
that we may receive your wisdom
and discern your guiding truth.
Open our hearts and minds
to love your teachings.
Transform our lives to walk in your ways,
that we may live our gratitude
in all that we do,
every hour of the day.

Proclamation and Response

Prayer of Confession (Ephesians 5, John 6)
God of mercy and compassion,
forgive our foolish ways.
When we are drunk with the foolishness of this world,
guide us back to your wisdom and truth.

When we seek after food that does not satisfy
    and teachings that confuse and misguide us,
        feed us instead from the bread
           of your life and love.
Forgive us; redeem us; and reclaim us,
    that we may walk with you all of our days.

Words of Assurance (Psalm 111, John 6)
God is full of mercy and compassion,
    giving food to all who yearn for the bread of life.
In the grace of Jesus Christ, we are filled
    with the bread of mercy and compassion,
    forgiven and reconciled with God.

Passing the Peace of Christ (Ephesians 5)
With songs of praise in our hearts and words of love on
our lips, let us share signs of peace and grace.

Prayer of Preparation (1 Kings 3, Ephesians 5)
God of wisdom and truth,
    give us discerning minds
        and understanding hearts,
           that we may hear your word
                and walk in your ways.

Response to the Word (Ephesians 5)
Be careful to live your life wisely.
    We will take every opportunity
    to understand and heed God's will.
Be filled with the Spirit of mercy and grace.
    We will speak to one another
    with songs of praise and hearts of love.
Give thanks to God for all things in all places.
    We will live our gratitude,

> by walking in God's ways
> and working in unity with one another.

Thanksgiving and Communion

Offering Prayer (Psalm 111, John 6)
> For your glorious deeds,
> **we give thanks and praise.**
> For your wondrous works,
> **we rejoice and celebrate this day.**
> With these gifts, may the world be fed.
> **We pray for your blessing and grace.**

Invitation to Communion (John 6)
> Come to the table of grace.
> Whoever comes to Jesus finds the bread of life.
> **We are empty and our needs are great.**
> Come to the table of grace.
> Whoever comes to Jesus will never thirst.
> **We are parched and thirst for the grace of God.**
> Come to the table of grace.
> Whoever comes to Jesus tastes eternal life.

Sending Forth

Benediction (Ephesians 6)
> Go in peace with love and faith.
> **May grace be with us forever!**

August 23, 2015

Thirteenth Sunday after Pentecost, Proper 16
B. J. Beu

Color

Green

Scripture Readings

1 Kings 8:(1, 6, 10-11) 22-30, 41-43; Psalm 84; Ephesians 6:10-20; John 6:56-69

Theme Ideas

With the exception of the reading from John, prayer is a unifying theme of these texts. Solomon prays at the dedication of the temple in Jerusalem. The psalmist prays for Israel and the joys of being in God's house. And Paul enjoins Christians to put on the full armor of God and pray in the Spirit at all times. To tie in the Gospel reading, worship leaders could show how communion and prayer in the Spirit allow us to abide in Christ.

Invitation and Gathering

Contemporary Gathering Words (Psalm 84, Ephesians 6)
Sing God's praises.
Dance and rejoice in God's splendor.
Pray without ceasing.
Laugh and rejoice in our God.

Call to Worship (Psalm 84)
How lovely is your dwelling place, O Lord of hosts!
To you our hearts sing for joy.
Happy are those who live and pray in your house.
Happy are those who find their strength in you.
It is better to be a doorkeeper in your house
than to live in the tents of wickedness.
We will dwell in God's courts forever.

Opening Prayer (1 Kings 8, Ephesians 6)
Eternal God,
there is none like you
in heaven or on earth.
If you will walk with us in faithful love,
we will walk in your paths
all the days of our lives.
As you filled Solomon's temple
with your glory and power,
so now fill our lives with your presence,
that we may find the strength
to live righteously
and resist the forces of evil. Amen.

Proclamation and Response

Prayer of Confession (1 Kings 8, Ephesians 6)
Guide and Guardian,

we pledge our loyalty to you,
    yet stray from your ways;
we proclaim the great deeds of the saints,
    yet fail to follow in their footsteps;
we confess you with our lips,
    yet deny you with our actions.
Forgive our reluctance
    to put on the full armor of faith
        and to live as you intend. Amen.

Words of Assurance (Psalm 84)

God is our protector and shield
    when we walk with upright hearts.
Trust in the Lord, and receive God's blessings.

Passing the Peace of Christ (Ephesians 6)

Put on Christ, our shield of faith, and share the gospel of peace with those around you.

Invitation to the Word (John 6)

When the crowds heard that to abide in Jesus, they had to partake of his body and blood, many turned and went away. Some teachings are difficult to bear. Yet, when we truly partake of Christ's presence, all things are possible. Listen for the word of God.

Response to the Word (Ephesians 6)

God's wisdom and power make us strong.
    God's compassion and love will be our armor.
God's righteousness and salvation help us pray.
    Christ's glory will be our shield.
God's wisdom and truth help us stand firm.
    The Spirit's fire will be our sword.
God's gospel of peace shows us the way.
    The love of God will be our traveling cloak.

Call to Prayer (Psalm 84, Ephesians 6)

The Lord of hosts hears our prayers. The God of Jacob and Solomon and Paul and Peter gives ear to our petitions and our songs of thanksgiving. Let us lift up our prayers to the One who is our strength and our shield.

Thanksgiving and Communion

Offering Prayer (Psalm 84)

Loving God,
>in your care,
>>even the sparrow finds a home,
>>even the robin finds a nest for herself;
>in your care,
>>even the least of us finds life and spirit;
>>even the lost among us find their way home.
In gratitude for all we have received,
>accept our gifts and offerings,
>>that we may abide in your love. Amen.

Sending Forth

Benediction (Ephesians 6)

Be strong in the Lord.
Draw strength from God's power.
>**We will put on the full armor of God.**
Stand boldly in God's truth.
Withstand the temptations of this world.
>**We will fasten the belt of truth around our waist,**
>**and put on the breastplate of justice.**

Rely on the shield of faith.
Put on the helmet of salvation.
    We will carry the sword of the Spirit
    and proclaim the gospel of peace.
Pray without ceasing and you will live.

August 30, 2015

Fourteenth Sunday after Pentecost, Proper 17
Mary Petrina Boyd

Color

Green

Scripture Readings

Song of Songs 2:8-13; Psalm 45:1-2, 6-9 (or Psalm 15); James 1:17-27; Mark 7:1-8, 14-15, 21-23

Theme Ideas

God's word invites us to delight in both creation and the love we have for one another. The psalmist knows that it is God who inspires the words of the pen that honor God's servant, the king. James speaks of the danger of angry words, invites us to listen to God's transforming word, and calls us to act upon God's word of freedom. Jesus rebukes those who speak empty words and calls people to live in ways that speak God's word of purity and love. The sensual delight of the Song of Songs and Psalm 45 remind us that joy is a gift from God. These scriptures also contain a deep call for justice. James reminds us that the deepest devotion to God is to care for those in need. Finally, these scriptures present a wonderful balance between being and doing. The sensual delights of the Song of Songs and the psalm speak of the gift of the senses to God's creatures. James and Mark invite us to act in ways that reflect God's love.

Invitation and Gathering

Contemporary Gathering Words (Song of Songs 2)
Rise up, my dearest, my fairest, and go!
Who is it that calls to us?
It is God who calls and beckons to us all.
What will we find?
We will hear the song of love,
and see beauty blooming all around us.
Let us delight in God's gifts!
Rise up, my dearest, my fairest, and go!
We go to praise our God!

Call to Worship (Song of Songs 2, James 1, Mark 7)
God calls to us, inviting us to revel in creation.
We come with joy, delighting in God's world!
God speaks words of life and hope.
We welcome God's word into our hearts.
God asks us to live God's word.
We worship God with all that we do!

—Or—

Call to Worship (James 1)
The Creator of the heavenly lights made us for this:
To care for one another and to do God's work.
The unchanging character of God will never fail.
We are the first crop of God's harvest.

Welcome God's word into your hearts!
We welcome God's transforming word!

—Or—

Call to Worship (Psalm 45)
A marvelous word stirs our hearts!
God is here!
God has blessed us forever.
God's word is eternal
God loves righteousness and hates wickedness.
The oil of gladness pours over us.
A marvelous word stirs our hearts!
God is here!

Opening Prayer (Song of Songs 2, James 1, Mark 7)
Creating God, you invite us into a world of delight.
Instead of rigid obedience to rules and regulations,
you desire the willing gift of our hearts.
As we bring our hearts to you in worship,
may the words we speak reveal your grace,
and may our actions embody your love.
Renew and create us anew
for your work in the world. Amen.

Proclamation and Response

Prayer of Confession (Song of Songs 2, James 1)
Creator, you call us to delight in your creation,
yet we are too busy to notice the beauty around us.
Eternal Word, you place your word within our hearts,
yet we fail to listen to your guidance.

Spirit of Truth, you call us to act with justice
  in all that we say and all that we do,
    yet we often fail to act on our good intentions.
Remake us into a community of love—
  a community that does your will
    and helps heal a world in need.

—*Or*—

Prayer of Confession (Mark 7)
God of compassion,
  we talk about being faithful to your love,
    while our hearts go after other desires.
Our love of you and of one another fails,
  while we devise complex rules and regulations
    to judge others.
We want to be yours,
  but harmful thoughts carry us away
    from your purposes.
Cleanse the meditations of our hearts,
  that our thoughts may reflect your goodness.
Keep us from envy, greed, and deceit,
  and remake us in the image of your love. Amen.

Words of Assurance (James 1)
God transforms our lives by the power of love,
  speaking words of truth to enlighten our spirits
  and leading us in the path of justice.

Passing the Peace of Christ (James 1)
Each of you is God's good harvest and has God's word
planted deep within. As you offer one another signs of
peace, recognize God's love in one another.

Introduction to the Word (James 1)
Welcome God's word. It is spoken in scripture. It is
planted within the heart. It has the power to save us

from all manner of evil. It has the power to bless the world. Welcome God's word.

Response to the Word (Psalm 45, James 1)
By your true word, you have given us life.
Your word stirs deep within us.
We welcome the transforming power of that word,
    as it leads us toward justice and righteousness.
Help us to become doers of your word,
    that we may be a blessing to others.

Thanksgiving and Communion

Invitation to the Offering (James 1, Mark 7)
Instead of rigid obedience to rules and regulations, God desires the willing gift of our hearts. We give not with words alone, but with all that we do. Let us bring our gifts to God, knowing that true devotion to God is shown by caring for those in need.

Offering Prayer (James 1)
Source of every good and perfect gift,
    you have given us all that we need.
We are the fruit of your love.
From the abundance of your love,
    we learn to give.
Use our gifts and use our lives:
    to care for those in need,
    to offer a listening ear,
    and to speak a word of comfort.
May our words and our actions reflect your love. Amen.

Invitation to Communion (James 1, Mark 7)
As we gather at Christ's table to eat, drink,
    and remember our loving friend and teacher,
    we do so in remembrance of him.

By these actions we are nourished for God's work.
As we do this we are fed by grace, blessed by love,
    and sent forth to live God's word.

Great Thanksgiving (Song of Songs 2, James 1, Mark 7)
Creator of the heavenly lights,
    your love does not change,
        for you are always faithful.
By your word you gave birth to creation,
    calling everything into being.
You invited us to live in a world of beauty and delight.
You spoke your presence in blooming flowers,
    singing birds, and fruit-laden trees.
You gave us a law of love,
    and planted your word deep inside us,
    that we might know your salvation.
Yet we ignored your word, holding on to rules
    created by humans, judging one another,
    speaking one thing, yet doing another.
Your word of love called us back.
So we sing our praise to you:
    Holy, holy, holy Lord, God of power and might,
        heaven and earth are full of your glory.
    Hosanna in the highest. Blessed is the one
        who comes in the name of the Lord.
    Hosanna in the highest.
Your word was born among us in Jesus.
He reminded us of the words of the prophet Isaiah:
    "The people honor me with their lips,
    but their hearts are far away from me."
Jesus called us to turn our hearts back to you.
He asked us to purify our lives
    and to live God's commandments.
This is God's perfect law, the law of freedom.

As he faced death, Jesus gathered his friends
    around your table.
Taking the bread in his hands,
    he blessed and broke it, and shared it saying:
    "Take and eat. I offer myself to you.
    Do this and remember."
Lifting the cup, he thanked you and blessed it,
    and shared it saying: "Take and drink.
    This is the gift of forgiveness.
    Do this and remember."
Blessed by your love, healed by your word,
    fed by your grace, we proclaim the mystery of faith:
    Christ has died.
    Christ is risen.
    Christ will come again.
Send your spirit upon these gifts:
    grapes of the vine, grain from the fields.
Transform them by your love
    into your nourishing presence in our lives.
Send your Spirit upon this community,
    that we may bear the fruits of your word of grace
    doing your word in acts of justice and righteousness.

We praise you, O God, not just with our lips,
    but with our lives, for you are the source of all that is,
      the word that sustains us,
        the Spirit that empowers us. Amen.

Sending Forth

Benediction (Song of Songs 2, James 1)
    Now that you have heard the word of God,
      be doers of the word planted deep within you.
    Be slow to speak, quick to listen, and slow to anger.
    Do this and you will be blessed.

September 6, 2015

Fifteenth Sunday after Pentecost, Proper 18
J. Wayne Pratt

Color

Green

Scripture Readings

Proverbs 22:1-2, 8-9, 22-23; Psalm 125; James 2:1-10
(11-13) 14-17; Mark 7:24-37

Theme Ideas

Woven into the thread of this week's readings is a simple fact: Barriers are consistently being broken down by Jesus—barriers of rich and poor, insider and outsider, body and spirit. God welcomes all, and we are called to do likewise. Another theme is the universal desire for healing and wholeness, and that God's healing embraces everyone. While it is necessary that we work for peace and justice, we must also recognize inner peace and communion with God and neighbor as equally important gifts. Faith in action is made manifest when we genuinely care for the least of these, the hurting, and the vulnerable. Healing gestures contribute to the wellness of the individual as well as the community, and reflect our faith in God.

Invitation and Gathering

Contemporary Gathering Words (James 2, Mark 12:31)

It is here in the sanctuary of our God
    that we learn to fulfill the royal law of God's Word:
    "Love your neighbor as yourself."
May our praise and worship this day,
    remind us of God's love, forgiveness,
    and healing grace.

Call to Worship (Psalm 125)

Those who place their trust in the Lord
are like Mount Zion, never shaken, lasting forever.
    Mountains surround the holy city of Jerusalem,
    and the Lord continually surrounds and protects
    God's people.
The Lord's favor is ever with those whose hearts
are in the right place.
    May peace be always with God's people!

—Or—

Call to Worship (James 2, Mark 7)

God is here in this place, calling all God's children
to worship with their whole lives.
    We come, bringing our faith made alive
    through works of love and mercy and liberation.
Come, trusting that God will always respond to our need.
    We come in trust and joy and faith and deeds.
(Joanne Carlson Brown)

Opening Prayer (Mark 7)

Creating, loving, and healing God,
    we gather together this day,
        coming from different places
        and situations in life.

In faith, we fall before you in praise and worship,
 desiring to be fed with your love
  and healed with your grace.
Fill us with wonder, O God,
 that we may proclaim your good news
  for all to hear.
Open up our ears, our mouths, and our hearts this day.
In Christ Jesus' name, we pray. Amen.

Proclamation and Response

Prayer of Confession (Proverbs 22, James 2)
God of mercy and justice,
 you call us to love our neighbors as ourselves,
  and to speak and act with mercy and grace.
Instead, we have been judgmental, played favorites,
 and turned away from the poor and needy.
We have failed to be impartial,
 and have abused our power.
Reframe and redirect our actions, Lord,
 that beauty, truth, and justice
  may prevail throughout your creation.
Help each one of us, Lord,
 to be rich in faith, love, and generosity.
In Jesus' name, we pray. Amen.

Words of Assurance (Proverbs 22, Psalm 125)
Mercy overrules judgment, love overcomes hatred,
 and God's embrace reaches out to all people,
 spanning all of the mountains and chasms
 that confront us.
Be at peace with yourselves and with others,
 knowing that God's mercy endures forever.

Passing the Peace of Christ (Proverbs 22)

Creating us all as equals, and calling us to be generous in our faith, the Lord invites us to offer gestures of welcome as we share the peace of Christ.

Introduction to the Word (Mark 7)

As we break open the word of God, let us also break open our hearts in ways that will allow us to receive the Good News. Let us pray.
May we feed upon your word, O God,
    as children of your kingdom.
And may it cleanse and renew us for worship
    and for service to your glory.
This is the word of our Lord.
Thanks be to God.

Response to the Word (Proverbs 22)

For many, it is easy and quite comfortable to esteem wealth over reputation. Silver and gold become more important to us than character and respect. Greed sows injustice and results in stealing from the poor. God challenges each one of us to live out the gospel message, sharing and caring and loving one another. May each one of us be inspired to defend and uphold those whom God has placed before us, pouring out grace and love to all God's children.

Thanksgiving and Communion

Invitation to the Offering (Proverbs 22)

God comes among us to bring healing, hope, and love of neighbor. So, too, the gifts we share bring joy and hope to God's children, breaking the bonds of evil, injustice, and oppression. Happy are God's generous people. Let us offer ourselves and our gifts to God.

Offering Prayer (Proverbs 22, Psalm 125)
    Transform these offerings, gracious and loving God,
        that they may:
            feed the hungry;
            remove the shackles of oppression;
            and bring peace, justice, and mercy,
                to those in need of your love and grace,
                both now and forevermore. Amen.

Sending Forth

Benediction (Proverbs 22, James 2, Mark 7)
    Go now in peace—
        loving one another in Christ's name.
    Go now with Christ Jesus—
        who healed the sick, the rich, and the poor,
        the saint and the sinner.
    Go now with the Holy Spirit—
        who comforts, inspires, and offers direction.
    Go now in peace—
        and may the loving embrace of our God
        be with you this day and forevermore. Amen.

September 13, 2015

Sixteenth Sunday after Pentecost, Proper 19
B. J. Beu

Color

Green

Scripture Readings

Proverbs 1:20-33; Psalm 19; James 3:1-12; Mark 8:27-38

Theme Ideas

Proverbs, James, and Mark offer this amazing insight: Willful people do foolish and destructive things that annoy God. In Proverbs, Dame Wisdom cries out to those who love being simple and whose actions are fraught with folly. When calamity strikes, she will laugh, for they have been warned. The epistle speaks of the dangers of gossip and errant teachings, warning that an unbridled tongue can unleash the very fires of hell. Mark's Gospel highlights Peter's big mistake of rebuking Jesus. Jesus rebukes Peter for setting his mind on worldly rather than on divine things. The psalmist proclaims that fear of the Lord is the beginning of wisdom.

Invitation and Gathering

Contemporary Gathering Words (Proverbs 1)
Wisdom speaks to us.
We will not shut out the lessons she teaches.
Wisdom cries out her warning.
We will not ignore her guidance.
Wisdom calls to us.
We will dwell in the house of the Lord forever.

Call to Worship (Psalm 19)
The heavens are telling the glory of God.
Day pours forth speech,
and night declares knowledge.
The law of the Lord is perfect,
reviving the soul.
The decrees of the Lord are sure,
making wise the simple.
More to be desired are they than gold.
Sing to the Wisdom of the ages.
Join the heavens in telling the glory of our God.

Opening Prayer (Proverbs 1, Psalm 19, Mark 8)
Eternal God,
the voice of the heavens
declares your glory
and rejoices in your precepts.
As we proclaim our faith in your Son,
help us embrace the more difficult journey
of turning our minds from human things
to focus on heavenly matters.
May we be found faithful
when Wisdom comes to call. Amen.

Proclamation and Response

Prayer of Confession (Proverbs 1, James 3)
> Wisdom of the Ages,
>> cry out in the streets once more,
>>> that we may hear your voice
>>> and amend our ways.
> For only fools hate knowledge,
>> and only the wayward delight in their scoffing.
> Save us from our foolish ways,
>> and bridle our lips,
>>> that our tongues may not speak evil
>>>> or utter falsehoods,
>>>>> words that poison the soul.
> Why do we use the same tongue
>> that praises your name
>>> to curse others who are made in your likeness?
> Forgive us, Holy One.
> Grant us self-control,
>> that our lives may bear the fruit
>>> of your righteousness. Amen.

Words of Assurance or Introduction to the Word (Psalm 19)
> The perfect law of God is sweeter than honey,
>> and far more precious than gold.
> It revives the soul and makes us whole.
> Hear the word this day
>> and be made whole once more.

Passing the Peace of Christ (Proverbs 1)
> Those who listen to Holy Wisdom will dwell secure and live at ease. With the blessings of God to lead us, let us share signs of Christ's peace with one another.

Introduction to the Word (Proverbs 1:1, 23)

Wisdom cries out in the street. In the square she raises her voice. Give heed to her reproof, for she will make her thoughts known to you. Listen for the word of God.

Response to the Word (Psalm 19:7-8 NRSV)

"The law of the LORD is perfect, reviving the soul;
the decrees of the LORD are sure,
making wise the simple;
the precepts of the LORD are right, rejoicing the heart;
the commandment of the LORD is clear,
enlightening the eyes."
This is the word of God for the people of God.
Thanks be to God!

Introduction to the Message (Psalm 19:14)

May the words of my mouth and the meditation of my heart be acceptable to you, O Lord, my rock and my redeemer.

Thanksgiving and Communion

Invitation to the Offering (Psalm 19)

The heavens are telling the glory of God. Let us join the heavenly firmament in singing God's praises. Let us live out our joy by sharing from our abundance to the glory of God.

Offering Prayer (Psalm 19)

Glorious God,
your teachings are more to be desired
than fine gold and precious jewels.
You have taught us to share your gifts
with those in need.

Transform these offerings into gifts for your world—
gifts that will bring hope and light, peace and love,
where they are needed most.
In Jesus' name, we pray. Amen.

Sending Forth

Benediction (Psalm 19, Mark 8)
May the words of our mouths
be acceptable and true.
May the meditations of our hearts
be loving and pure.
May the actions of our lives
be compassionate and just.
May the wisdom of our God
bless us and keep us,
now and forevermore. Amen.

September 20, 2015

Seventeenth Sunday after Pentecost, Proper 20
Deborah Sokolove

Color

Green

Scripture Readings

Proverbs 31:10-31; Psalm 1; James 3:13–4:3, 7-8a; Mark 9:30-37 ˙

Theme Ideas

True wisdom is found in service to others, in generosity of spirit, and in doing the work that God calls us to do. The fruit of true wisdom is peacefulness, gentleness, and righteousness. The Holy One is close to those who seek God.

Invitation and Gathering

Contemporary Gathering Words (Psalm 1, James 3–4)
Who is wise and understanding among us?
Who is able to make room for God in our midst?
As we draw near to God, God draws near to us.

Call to Worship (Psalm 1, James 3–4)
> Who is wise and understanding among us?
> > **Those who do not follow the advice of the wicked**
> > **or take the path that sinners tread.**
> > **Those who do not sit in the seat of scoffers.**
> Our delight is in the teachings of the Holy One,
> meditating day and night on the word of God.
> > **As we draw near to God, God draws near to us.**

Opening Prayer (Psalm 1, James 3–4, Mark 9)
> God of wisdom and grace,
> > you call us to be servants to all,
> > > and to welcome strangers and children
> > > > in your name.
> You call us to be men and women of valor,
> > and to do what is right and worthy,
> > > without thought of reward.
> Help us to delight in your word,
> > and to live in your peace,
> > > that we may be known as your people. Amen.

Proclamation and Response

Prayer of Confession (James 3–4, Mark 9)
> Loving God, you teach us that those who would be first
> > must be servants to all.
> > **Yet we live our lives,**
> > > **with bitter envy and selfish ambition**
> > > > **in our hearts.**
> Our cravings cause disputes and conflicts among us.
> > **We convince ourselves that material possessions**
> > > **will bring us peace.**
> Our pride makes us blind to the needs of others.

We seek our own pleasure,
>> imagining that what we want is what we need.
Forgive, Holy One,
>> when we refuse to submit our lives
>>> to wisdom's correction and guidance.

Words of Assurance (James 3–4)
> God has shown us the path to true wisdom,
>> drawing near to us when we draw near to God.
> In the name of Christ, you are forgiven.
> **In the name of Christ, you are forgiven.**
> **Glory to God. Amen.**

Passing the Peace of Christ (Psalm 1, James 3–4)
> In making peace with one another, we draw near to God.
> The peace of Christ be with you.
> **The peace of Christ be with you always.**

Response to the Word (Proverbs 31, James 3–4)
> Like the woman of valor, whose works praise her wordlessly in the eyes of the city, let us live our days with gentleness born of wisdom.

Thanksgiving and Communion

Invitation to the Offering (Proverbs 31)
> Opening our hands to those in need, let us bring our gifts and offerings.

Offering Prayer (Psalm 1)
> God of wisdom and grace,
>> accept the fruit of our labor
>>> as signs of our delight in your word. Amen.

Great Thanksgiving
> Christ be with you.
> **And also with you.**

Lift up your hearts.
> **We lift them up to God.**
Let us give our thanks to the Holy One.
> **It is right to give our thanks and praise.**

It is a right, good, and a joyful thing,
> always and everywhere to give our thanks to you,
> who have given us your holy word,
> and taught us the ways of wisdom and peace.
We give you thanks for true wisdom,
> for the laws of righteousness
> that keep us as steady as trees
> planted by streams of water,
> yielding fruit in their season.
And so, with your creatures on earth
> and all the heavenly chorus,
> we praise your name and join their unending hymn:
> **Holy, holy, holy Lord, God of power and might,**
> > **heaven and earth are full of your glory.**
> **Hosanna in the highest. Blessed is the one**
> > **who comes in the name of the Lord.**
> **Hosanna in the highest.**
Holy are you, and holy is your child, Jesus Christ,
> who taught us that those who wish to be first
> must be last and servant of all.

On the night in which he gave himself up,
> Jesus took bread, gave thanks to you,
> broke the bread, and gave it to the disciples, saying:
> "Take, eat; this is my body which is given for you.
> Do this in remembrance of me."

When the supper was over, Jesus took the cup,
>   offered thanks and gave it to the disciples, saying:
>   "Drink from this, all of you;
>   this is my life in the new covenant,
>   poured out for you and for many,
>   for the forgiveness of sins.
>   Do this, as often as you drink it,
>   in remembrance of me."
And so, in remembrance of your mighty acts
>   in Jesus Christ, we proclaim the mystery of faith.
>   **Christ has died.**
>   **Christ is risen.**
>   **Christ will come again.**
Pour out your Holy Spirit on us,
>   and on these gifts of bread and wine.
Make them be for us the body and blood of Christ,
>   that we may be the body of Christ
>   to a world that longs for peace.

God of wisdom and grace, Spirit of gentleness,
>   Servant of all, we praise your holy, eternal,
>   loving name. Amen.

Sending Forth

Benediction (Psalm 1, James 3-4, Mark 9)
>   Go into the world with gentleness and peace.
>   Be willing to yield to the will of God,
>   welcoming strangers and children
>   in the name of Christ.
>   The God of wisdom and grace will be near you,
>   spreading mercy and goodness wherever you go.
>   Amen.

September 27, 2015

Eighteenth Sunday after Pentecost, Proper 21
Safiyah Fosua

Color
Green

Scripture Readings
Esther 7:1-6, 9-10; 9:20-22; Psalm 124; James 5:13-20; Mark 9:38-50

Theme Ideas
In this week's Hebrew Scripture reading, Esther lived in the shadow of genocide and oppression. But God *interrupted* the flow of events and historians record a surprise ending to her story. How many times have we whispered the refrain of the psalmist: *"If it had not been the LORD who was on our side…"*(v. 1a NRSV)? This week, we join Esther in celebrating the special times when God intervenes in our lives.

Invitation and Gathering

Contemporary Gathering Words
(Stream or loop words on screen with an all-black background and simple bold font, while peaceful music plays in the background.)

Sometimes, when life is speaking harshly and cruelly...
God interrupts and insists upon having the last word.

Call to Worship (Psalm 124)

If it had not been for the Lord who was on our side:
when the weather patterns changed
and tornados, hurricanes, and wildfires
came out of nowhere...

If it had not been for the Lord who was on our side:
when the flood waters came into our homes
and flooded our fields...

If it had not been for the Lord who was on our side:
when life happened, and things did not go as we
planned...

Where would we be?
How would we make it through?

Let us worship the One who is always on our side.

Opening Prayer (Psalm 124:1a, NRSV)

God, when we hear the daily news,
it is easy to think that life is a valley of sorrows
filled with tears.
Remind us through the stories of survivors,
that you are with us always
and that your love for us never fails.
We celebrate the times when heaven and earth meet—
the times you break into our lives
in ways that make us exclaim:
If it had not been for the Lord
who was on our side...!
Thank you for a love that transcends calamity—
a love that lifts up those who suffer,
a love that frees the lips to rejoice. Amen.

Proclamation and Response

Prayer of Confession (Esther 7)

Merciful God,
    it is foolish to presume that you will intervene
        every time we are in trouble,
            but sometimes we do.
We live as though misery
    should never find our home address,
        that sorrow should never sit at our doorstep.
Forgive us, God, for those times:
    we have taken you for granted;
    we have taken credit for your interventions;
    we have blamed you, blamed one another,
        or even blamed ourselves
            for the suffering in our world.
Forgive us, God,
    and teach us how to weep with those who weep
        and to rejoice with those who rejoice.
(A time of silence may follow.)

Words of Assurance (James 5)

Emmanuel! God is with us!
Hear the good news: God does not abandon us,
    but stays ever hopeful that we will realize our sins,
    confess them, and be healed.
In the name of Jesus Christ, you are forgiven.

Response to the Word (Esther 7)

God, we have heard the story of Esther.
Grant that we may have her courage
    when you call us to stand up
        for justice and mercy.

May we be steadfast in faith,
  and strong in resolve and action,
    when you call upon us
      to make a stand for what is right! Amen.

Thanksgiving and Communion

Introduction to the Offering (Esther 7)
Today, on this Sunday when Esther is remembered, we are reminded that we too are called upon to make sacrifices for the work of God.

Offering Prayer (Esther 7)
God, receive these monetary sacrifices
  and make us mindful of other sacrifices
    that we are called to make
      to further your work in the world. Amen.

Sending Forth

Benediction (Esther 7)
Today, we have been jarred and disturbed
  by the extraordinary courage of a young girl.
She did what she was able to do,
  and God intervened to save her people.
As you leave this place,
  be alert for what you are able to do
  on behalf of others.
Be alert, for God is fond of interrupting history
  and having the last word!
Go, in peace. Amen.

October 4, 2015

Nineteeneth Sunday after Pentecost, Proper 22/
World Communion Sunday

B. J. Beu

[Copyright © 2014 by B. J. Beu. Used by permission.]

Color

Green

Scripture Readings

Job 1:1; 2:1-10; Psalm 26 (or Psalm 8); Hebrews 1:1-4; 2:5-12; Mark 10:2-16

Theme Ideas

The readings from Job and Psalm 26 are a celebration of faith and integrity during times of trial. God boasts of Job's integrity, proclaiming him to be a blameless and upright man—even after Satan had devastated his family, his livelihood, and his health. Job illustrates that suffering is no indication of whether one has lived a godly life. The psalmist brags of personal integrity, challenging God to put this integrity to the test. Hebrews speaks of Christ's integrity and how he was made higher than the angels because of his faithfulness. The gospel reading does not fit with the other texts, and deals with marriage, divorce, adultery, and entering the kingdom of God like children.

Invitation and Gathering

Contemporary Gathering Words (Job 1-2)
Job was an upright man, blameless before God.
Then why was he stricken?
God's ways are hard to understand.
But God loved him still?
God loved Job still.
Why, why, why do the innocent suffer?
God's ways are hard to understand.
May we be as faithful as Job,
when suffering and evil befall us.

Call to Worship (Job 1-2, Psalm 26)
In this world of hardship and pain,
we will walk humbly before the Lord.
In a time when the pious struggle to make ends meet,
we will walk faithfully before our God.
In this world of hardship and pain,
we will walk humbly before the Lord.

Opening Prayer (Hebrews 1, Mark 10)
Almighty God,
long ago, you spoke to our ancestors
through the words of your prophets;
but today, you speak to us through a Son.
Help us become like children again,
and rejoice in your kingdom,
even as we seek to walk in your ways,
and trust in your Spirit. Amen.

Proclamation and Response

Prayer of Confession (Job 1–2, Psalm 26)
Holy God,
>   when the road of life is smooth,
>>   it is easy to remain faithful;
>   but when life becomes rough,
>>   we quickly fall away from you.
> Give us the faith of Jesus,
>   who taught his disciples to pray
>>   that they may be spared
>>>   from the time of trial.
> May our faithfulness be our words,
>   that others may see in our example
>>   the joys of an upright heart,
>>>   whether we are receiving
>>>>   the good from your hand,
>>>>>   or the bad. Amen.

Words of Assurance (Hebrews 2)
All who are sanctified by God
>   have the same Mother and Father.
> For this reason, Jesus is not ashamed
>   to call us brothers and sisters.
> As Christ's sisters and brothers,
>   rejoice in God's saving love.

Invitation to the Word (Hebrews 1–2)
Long ago, God spoke to our ancestors through the prophets. Today, God speaks to us through a Son, who is the very Word of God. As we hear the words of the prophets, may we listen for the teachings of the incarnate Word of God's unfailing love.

Response to the Word (Job 1–2, NRSV)

Job's wife derided her husband, "Do you still persist in your integrity? Curse God, and die." But Job responded, "Shall we receive the good at the hand of God, and not receive the bad?" As we move through life and seek to maintain our faith and integrity, let us be prepared to receive from God's hand, the bad along with the good.

Thanksgiving and Communion

Offering Prayer

God of love,
> send your Holy Spirit upon us.
Bless these gifts, touched by your Spirit,
> that they may be signs of life and love
>> to a world in need. Amen.

—Or—

Offering Prayer (Job 1–2)

God of whirlwind and fire,
> your ways are not our ways,
> your judgments are as high above us
>> as the stars are above the sea.
We joyfully receive the blessings of your hands,
> but shrink from the evils and setbacks in life.
Accept our offerings this day,
> that they may be a blessing
>> for those in need. Amen.

Invitation to Communion (World Communion Sunday)

Come to the table, you who are scattered and torn.
Here we find hope.

Come to the table, you who are scared and lonely.
Here we find love.
Come to the table, you who are tired and tense.
Here we find rest for our souls,
and food for our journey.
Come to the table, you who are lost and are searching.
Here we discover guidance,
and light for our darkness.
Come to the table, you who are happy or sad.
Here our lives are embraced by God's grace.

Great Thanksgiving

We give you thanks, our creator and liberator,
for by your Word you have called forth creation,
you have created us in your image.
You led us from slavery to freedom,
going ever before us
with cloud and fiery pillar.
With burning coals you gave utterance to the prophets,
to demand that justice roll down like waters,
and righteousness like an ever-flowing stream.
In the fullness of time, your spirit descended
like a dove upon Jesus, anointing him:
to preach good news to the poor,
to proclaim release to the captives,
to offer recovery of sight to the blind,
to set at liberty those who were oppressed,
and to declare the reign of God in our midst.
When Jesus gathered with those whom he loved,
he was known to them in the breaking of bread.
Before feeding the multitudes,
he broke bread and gave thanks.

When two or three were gathered together,
    he broke bread and gave thanks.
He sought the outcasts and broke bread with them,
    witnessing the fullness of your grace.
(Joanne Brown)

Words of Institution
    On the night of his greatest trial, he gathered his friends
        together in an upper room and said to them:
"Tonight, I am going to create
    a sustaining community among you.
It will not require you to always be faithful,
    or perfect, or good, or right, or powerful,
    or unblemished, or pure.
It will not require you to hold an advanced degree
    or to have the proper wealth, skin color,
    sexual identity, gender, or religion.
This community we are creating tonight,
    requires two things:
    your willingness to share with one another,
    and your remembrance of me.
These two are enough to bind you to one another,
    and to your work on behalf of the world."
(Joanne Brown)

Words of Consecration
Jesus said: "Take this bread, the bread of life:
    It represents my physical presence,
    which has been with you on many adventures,
    and the bodies of all who have tried to love mercy,
    create justice, and build the kingdom of God
    on earth.
Whenever you eat bread, remember this evening.
Think on what we have tried to do for the poor
    and those who are marginalized.

Take this cup, the cup of salvation:
>   It represents the covenant we make
>   with one another to always be there for one another;
It also represents my promise to be with you always.
This cup and your thoughts of me will sustain you
>   and restore your spirits."
(Joanne Brown)

Invitation

As we break this bread and drink this cup,
>   we do so remembering a life lived in thanksgiving—
>   a life of uncompromising commitment
>   to justice and equality, a life that led
>   to an unjust death on a cross.
And in the darkness of night, when evil and betrayal
>   seemed victorious, your creative power
>   burst upon us in the glory of the resurrection.
In remembering all that Jesus did and taught,
>   we wait with hope for the coming of God's reign
>   to bring peace and justice.
(Joanne Brown)

Giving the Bread and Cup

(The bread and wine are given to the people, with these or other words of blessing.)
Take and eat. May you never cease to hunger for justice.
Take and drink. May you never cease to thirst for mercy.
(Joanne Brown)

Sending Forth

Benediction (World Communion Sunday)

As you have refreshed us at your table,
weave us together as one body, one people.

As you have shared your sacred meal with us,
　　strengthen us, that we may be united in faith.
As you have blessed us with your loving presence,
　　send us forth in courage and peace,
　　rejoicing in the power of your Spirit.
(Joanne Brown and B. J. Beu)

October 11, 2015

Twentieth Sunday after Pentecost, Proper 23
Joanne Carlson Brown

Color

Green

Scripture Readings

Job 23:1-9, 16-17; Psalm 22:1-15; Hebrews 4:12-16; Mark 10:17-31

Theme Ideas

Today's scriptures tell of people who feel that God has abandoned them and people who have abandoned God. These passages are heavy with bitterness and disappointment. But even in these passages, there is a sense of God's presence and possibilities. Rather than shying away from the challenges these texts present, our challenge is to help people understand that God is with them when they are experiencing a "dark night of the soul."

Invitation and Gathering

Contemporary Gathering Words (Job 23, Psalm 22, Hebrews 4, Mark 10)
Is God hiding from us?
Surely God is testing us.

God makes impossible demands.

God's words pierce our souls.

Yet, all is not doom and gloom.

From the womb, God cares for us.

Really?

God is there for us forever. This is a promise.

Let us worship our God

for whom nothing is impossible.

Call to Worship (Job 23, Psalm 22, Mark 10)

God is holy and worthy of praise.

Our ancestors trusted God

and were delivered in their time of need.

Although we often feel alone and tested,

God has cared for us from the womb.

Come. Let us worship a God of infinite possibilities
and boundless love.

Opening Prayer (Job 23, Psalm 22, Hebrews 4, Mark 10)

O God, our God,

sometimes we feel that you are hiding from us;

sometimes we feel that you demand too much;

sometimes we feel challenged beyond endurance.

In this time of worship,

may we hear not only words of challenge,

but also words of comfort and promise.

May we see that Jesus understands our needs

and what we are going through;

and in this seeing,

may we find hope and grace

in times of need. Amen.

Proclamation and Response

Prayer of Confession (Job 23, Psalm 22, Hebrews 4, Mark 10)
Where are you, God?
Why have you abandoned me?
Why are you placing obstacles in our way?
Why do you demand so much?
Forgive us, O God,
    when we dwell on these negative questions.
Help us see that you are with us always
    and always have been.
From the womb you have kept watch over us.
Forgive us when we doubt whether you really care for us
    or if you even exist at all.
Help us to see you, to experience you,
    and to feel your love. Amen.

Words of Assurance (Hebrews 4)
We do not worship one who is unable to sympathize
    with our weakness, but one who in every respect
    has been tested as we have.
Approach the throne of grace with boldness,
    knowing that you will receive mercy and forgiveness
    in the times of need.
Thanks be to God!

Passing the Peace of Christ (Mark 10)
Turn to those around you and say:
For God all things are possible.

Introduction to the Word
We have heard words that are hard to hear, and we have
heard words of grace and promise. May both words
touch our hearts and speak to us, for both lead to life.

Response to the Word (Mark 10)
> For the word that challenges our faithfulness;
> for the word that tests our resolve;
> for the word that promises life in the midst of death,
> **we offer our thanks to God.**

Thanksgiving and Communion

Invitation to the Offering (Job 23, Psalm 22, Hebrews 4, Mark 10)
> There are times when we feel abandoned by God. Perhaps this is one of those times for you. Be assured that God is here, and has loved us from the very beginning of our lives. There are many in the world who feel abandonment and doubt. Our offering this morning will enable this church to reach out in understanding, and to speak the word of hope and love and care that this world so desperately needs to hear. Our morning offering will now be received.

Offering Prayer (Job 23, Psalm 22, Hebrews 4, Mark 10)
> We come to the throne of grace
> > to offer ourselves and our material resources,
> > > trusting in your promises, O God.
> Receive our offerings,
> > especially our fears and doubts and questions,
> > > that we may be made whole again
> > > > through your love and mercy. Amen.

Sending Forth

Benediction (Job 23, Psalm 22, Hebrews 4, Mark 10)
> Even in the midst of doubts, questions, and testing,
> > God is with us always.

Even in times of trial,
    Jesus understands what we are going through
    and is with us through it all.
Even when we feel abandoned and alone,
    the Spirit comforts us with words of mercy,
    grace, and love.
Go, proclaiming: With God, all things are possible.

October 18, 2015

Twenty-first Sunday after Pentecost, Proper 24
B. J. Beu

[Copyright © 2014 by B. J. Beu. Used by permission.]

Color

Green

Scripture Readings

Job 38:1-7 (34-41); Psalm 104:1-9, 24, 35c; Hebrews 5:1-10; Mark 10:35-45

Theme Ideas

Great is God's power. God stretches the heavens like a tent, sets the earth on firm foundations, and covers the waters of the deep. We long for a taste of this power, unless we get caught in the whirlwind like Job. We long to possess this power, but Christ reminds us that true power is found in service. To embrace Christ's glory and sit at his right hand is to hang with thieves, to dine with sinners, to serve tirelessly. Job was a faithful follower of his God, yet he was not spared calamity. Christ's disciples are invited to drink the cup that Jesus drank, and to be baptized into his suffering and death. Is it any wonder more people do not flock to churches that truly preach the gospel? Yet, this is our road and the nature of true power. For when we follow in Christ's steps, serve with generosity, live with kindness, walk with humility, care with compassion, and serve in Christ's name, God draws us to Christ's side and clothes us with the greatest power and glory of all—the power and glory of love.

Invitation and Gathering

Contemporary Gathering Words (Job 38, Psalm 104, Mark 10)
As a lion pursues its prey,
    seek the Lord.
As the parched ground thirsts for rain,
    thirst for God.
As the morning star sang at creation,
    sing to the Lord.
As a drowning sailor reaches for a lifeline,
    take Christ's hand.

Call to Worship (Job 38, Psalm 104)
Bless the Lord, my soul,
and bless God's holy name.
    Bless God in the heavens,
    stretched out like a tent.
Bless God in the winds,
whispering words of life and love.
    Bless God in fire and flame,
    dancing with hues of orange and red.
Bless the Lord, my soul,
and bless God's holy name.

Opening Prayer (Job 38, Psalm 104, Mark 10)
God of power and might,
    blow through our lives

like a mighty whirlwind,
upsetting our complacency
and self-centered ways.
Shake our sunny conviction of your favor,
and rebuke our cavalier treatment
of friends and neighbors in need.
Clothe us with your love,
that we may be a people of hope,
a people of prayer,
and a people of true spirit,
through Christ, our Lord. Amen.

Proclamation and Response

Prayer of Confession (Job 38, Mark 10)

How often do we protest our righteousness, O God?
How often do we sit down to lick our wounds,
rather than embracing the evils in life
along with the good?
How easily we forget that Job was blameless
when he found himself in the path of the tornado.
How quickly we demand answers
to questions that have no answers.
How frequently we darken counsel
with words without knowledge or wisdom.
Forgive us, Lord.
Forgive us when we seek power over service,
and personal glory over humility.
Forgive us when we seek to sit at your right hand,
rather than accept the place of the servant.
Answer us in your whirlwind once more, Holy One.
It is enough to stand in the power and glory
of your awe and majesty. Amen.

Words of Assurance (Hebrews 5)
Christ, our High Priest, was made perfect
through his faithfulness in the face of pain and death.
In Jesus Christ, we are offered forgiveness in his name,
and fullness of grace.

Passing the Peace of Christ (Hebrews 5)
In the name of Christ, the begotten child of God, let us
turn to one another with joy, and share signs of God's
peace.

Introduction to the Word (Job 38)
We who have so many questions for our God must be
prepared to answer some ourselves. As today's scriptures are read, prayerfully reflect on what God is inquir-
ing of us in the reading. Listen for the word of God.

Response to the Word (Job 38, Psalm 104)
Merciful God,
you promise to put wisdom in our inward parts,
and to grant understanding to our minds.
How then do we so often fail to understand your ways?
Give us the wisdom to discern your will
in every moment of our lives.
Grant us the strength to drink from your cup
and to be baptized with your baptism,
that our lives may be lived in service to others.

Thanksgiving and Communion

Offering Prayer (Psalm 104:1-2, Mark 10)
Mighty God,
you are clothed with honor and majesty,
wrapped in light as with a garment.

You bring rain to the earth
    and food to your creatures.
We thank you for the abundance of our lives,
    and we praise you for the opportunity
        to share with others
            the bounty of your hand.
As we present these gifts,
    we dedicate our lives into your service. Amen.

Sending Forth

Benediction (Mark 10)
    Bless us, O God.
        **Bless us with a hunger
        to make a difference in the world.**
    Bless us, beloved Son.
        **Bless us with a kind and healing touch
        to comfort the afflicted.**
    Bless us, Great Spirit.
        **Bless us with the grace
        to live lives of meaning and purpose.**
    Bless us, O God.
        For we are your beloved children.

October 25, 2015

Twenty-second Sunday after Pentecost, Proper 25/Reformation Sunday

Mary J. Scifres

[Copyright © 2014 by Mary J. Scifres. Used by permission.]

Color

Green

Scripture Readings

Job 42:1-6, 10-17; Psalm 34:1-8 (19-22); Hebrews 7:23-28; Mark 10:46-52

Theme Ideas

The healing of Bartimaeus in Mark's Gospel offers many themes: the cry for mercy, the call of Christ, the cry for what we need from God, and the power of faith. As we cry out for mercy and for the things we need from God, God hears our cries, and offers the hand of healing and grace. For Job, this healing came after much suffering. For the psalmist, lament and joy ebb and flow throughout all of life. In Hebrews, we are promised that our perfect High Priest, Christ Jesus, has already imparted the gift of grace—a grace that always responds when we cry out for intercession and forgiveness. Bartimaeus encounters the challenging truth of this promise when

Jesus calls to him, invites him to claim his needs, and then heals him by the power of Bartimaeus's own faith.

Invitation and Gathering

Contemporary Gathering Words (Mark 10)
Take heart. Christ hears our cries,
and invites us into God's presence.
Take heart. Get up and worship the Lord,
for Christ is calling us now!

Call to Worship (Psalm 34, Mark 10)
Come and bless the Lord.
We come to seek God's grace.
Christ hears our every cry.
We need God's healing touch.
Take heart; have faith, for Christ has called us here.
We come to bless the Lord!

Opening Prayer (Mark 10)
Jesus, Son of David,
hear us as we call to you this day.
Speak to us in this holy time.
Enter our lives and heal our hurts,
that we may hear your truth
and trust in your grace.
Claim us as your own,
that we may go forth in the wholeness of faith.

Proclamation and Response

Prayer of Confession (Mark 10)
Jesus, child of God, hear our cries.
Have mercy on us.

Grant us your grace,
for we are broken and blind in so many ways.
(Silent confession may follow.)
Jesus, child of God, hear our cries.
Have mercy on us.
Grant us your grace,
that we may know your healing touch
and be restored to the fullness of life
in your holy name. Amen.

Words of Assurance (Psalm 34, Hebrews 7)
Taste and see that God is good.
In Christ Jesus, God is able to save us, to heal us,
to reconcile us with one another and with God.

Response to the Word: Invitation to Healing and Grace (Mark 10)
Come forth, all who are broken and torn.
Take heart, get up, for Christ is calling us
to healing and hope.
(Worshipers may be invited to come forward for anointing with oil and/or for prayer and blessing.)

Response to the Word: A Healing Blessing for All (Mark 10)
Take heart and go forth, for in Christ Jesus,
your faith has made you well!

Thanksgiving and Communion

Invitation to the Offering (Job 42, Hebrews 7, Mark 10)
As God has restored our fortunes with the grace of Jesus Christ, so now may we restore the fortunes of others through our gifts of love, compassion, and grace.

Offering Prayer (Psalm 34, Mark 10)
    We bless you, O God,
            as we offer these gifts back to you
                in your holy church.
    Even as we magnify your name,
            magnify these gifts,
                that they may bless and heal others
                    in your holy name. Amen.

Sending Forth

Benediction (Mark 10)
    Go forth with the blessing of God.
    Go forth with the healing of Christ.
    Go forth with the grace of the Holy Spirit.
    Go forth with the hope of faith.

November 1, 2015

All Saints Day/Twenty-third Sunday after Pentecost, Proper 26

B. J. Beu

[Copyright © 2014 by B. J. Beu. Used by permission.]

Color

White

Scripture Readings

ALL SAINTS DAY: Isaiah 25:6-9; Psalm 24; Revelation 21:1-6a; John 11:32-44

23rd SUNDAY AFTER PENTECOST: Ruth 1:1-18; Psalm 146; Hebrews 9:11-14; Mark 12:28-34

Theme Ideas

All Saints Day celebrates those who have died in the faith. Today's scripture readings reference the end time when there will be a new heaven and a new earth—a time when God will wipe away every tear. It is a time to celebrate the heavenly banquet, a banquet with rich food and well-aged wine. It is a time when weeping and mourning will be no more. The story of Jesus raising

Lazarus from the dead is a sign of God's power, even over death itself. The message is clear and unambiguous: The saints of God have nothing to fear from the grave.

(These Theme Ideas are for All Saints Day only. Theme Ideas and worship materials for the Twenty-third Sunday after Pentecost/Proper 26 may be found in the November 4 entry of The Abingdon Worship Annual 2012 *edition. That entry may also be found in the online materials for this resource.)*

Invitation and Gathering

Contemporary Gathering Words (Psalm 24, Revelation 21)
Lift up your heads, O gates!
Be lifted up, O ancient doors!
The King of glory has come.
God will wipe away every tear.
Mourning and death shall be no more.
For the first things have passed away.
Lift up your heads, O gates!
Be lifted up, O ancient doors!
The King of glory has come.

Call to Worship (Isaiah 25, Psalm 24)
Look, here is our God,
the One we have waited for.
Let us be glad and rejoice in our salvation.
Come feast on rich food and dine on fine wine.
Enjoy the blessings of the Lord,
the vindication from our God.
Come! Let us worship the Lord.

Opening Prayer (Isaiah 25, Psalm 24, Revelation 21)
God of new beginnings,
 you are the Alpha and the Omega,
  the beginning and the end of all things.
Remove the shroud that separates us
 from your mighty presence,
  that we may see you as you are.
Wipe away our tears
 and take away our disgrace,
  that we may come before your throne
   with hearts full of song
    and souls ablaze with joy.
Help us to live as those who are prepared to die,
 and enable us to die as those who go forth to live,
  so that whether living or dying,
   our hearts will always belong to you. Amen.

Proclamation and Response

Prayer of Confession (Psalm 24, Revelation 21, John 11)
Wellspring of tears,
 you know well our grief
  and our longing to see you face to face.
O how we wish you would come down and save us.
In our pain, we have grown impatient.
In our sorrow, we have doubted the depth of your love.
Forgive us, patient one,
 when we forget that Jesus wept
  at the death of his friend, Lazarus.
Renew our faithfulness, Holy One,
 when like Mary and Martha before us,
  we despair of tasting the joy of eternal life.

Open our mouths to exclaim with delight:
 Here is our God for whom we have waited!
We need your grace to complete us.
We need your love to make us whole. Amen.

Words of Assurance (Isaiah 25, Revelation 21)
The one who shows us a vision
 of a new heaven and a new earth is faithful.
The one who prepares for us
 a banquet of rich food and fine wines,
 will wipe away every tear.
The King of glory has come to bring us salvation.

Passing the Peace of Christ (Isaiah 25, Revelation 21)
God is here to wipe away every tear, and bring us blessing upon blessing. Let us rejoice in the fellowship of
the saints of God, as we share signs of peace in Christ's
name.

Introduction to the Word (Revelation 21)
The word of God is trustworthy and true. Listen for the
word of God.

Response to the Word (Isaiah 25, John 11)
God promises that those who believe will see the glory of God. On this day when we celebrate the life and
faith of the saints of God, renew our faith in the one for
whom we have waited.

Thanksgiving and Communion

Offering Prayer (Isaiah 25, Revelation 21)
God of abundance,
 you offer us rich food and fine wines;

you bless us with all the bounty
of your heavenly banquet.
May the gifts we offer this day,
provide food and drink to those who go without,
that all may come to know
the blessings of your table,
in this world and in the world to come.

Sending Forth

Benediction (Psalm 24, Revelation 21)
With clean hands and pure hearts,
hold fast to the faith of the saints who went before us.
In our living and in our dying, we belong to God.
With hopeful hearts and expectant spirits,
receive the blessings of our gracious host.
In our living and in our dying, we belong to God.
With Christ as our door to eternal life,
find the courage to open the door and go in.
In our living and in our dying, we belong to God.

November 8, 2015

Twenty-fourth Sunday after Pentecost, Proper 27
Mary J. Scifres

[Copyright © 2014 by Mary J. Scifres. Used by permission.]

Color

Green

Scripture Readings

Ruth 3:1-5; 4:13-17; Psalm 127 (or Psalm 146); Hebrews 9:24-28; Mark 12:38-44

Theme Ideas

The characters in today's scriptures model the value of giving all that they have—an uncommon value in today's world. Ruth gives her life and her future to her mother-in-law, as she follows Naomi back to her homeland, and then Ruth gives even her son so that Naomi may nurse and raise him as her own. In doing so, Ruth (and Naomi) give to the Hebrew people the grandfather of King David, and to Christians the ancestor of our savior Jesus. Jesus observes a poor widow who is giving all that she has to the temple treasury, and reminds us that giving everything is the blessing God seeks from us. The psalmist reminds us that only houses (and lives)

247

built by God will stand the test of time, and the test of worth. Giving everything we have puts us "all in." Only by doing so can we complete God's work, and be fully committed to following Christ. When we do so, the lives we build are both blessed and a blessing.

Invitation and Gathering

Contemporary Gathering Words (Psalm 127, Mark 12)
> What have you built lately: A house, a family,
>> a bank account, a church, a life?
> Unless God builds with us,
>> our building will amount to nothing.
> But when God builds, when we co-create with God,
>> our lives and our creations are God's lives,
>> God's creations.
> As we gather this day, God calls us to give
>> all that we have and all that we are.
> Whether out of poverty or out of abundance,
>> gifts given completely and generously
>> build the house of God!

Call to Worship (Psalm 127, Mark 12)
> Come to God's house with your songs and prayers.
>> **We lift our voices to God.**
> Come to God's house with your hopes and joys.
>> **We bring our thanks and praise.**
> Come to God's house with your needs and fears.
>> **We lay down our burdens before Christ.**
> Come to God's house with your gifts and treasures.
>> **We offer our lives to Christ.**
> Come to God's house with all that you have
> and with all that you are.
>> **Let us worship together this day.**

Opening Prayer (Mark 12)
> God of abundant love,
>> pour your love and your Spirit upon us,
>>> that we may recognize our abundance
>>>> and give our love and our lives
>>>>> completely and freely to you.
> In Christ's holy name, we pray. Amen.

Proclamation and Response

Prayer of Confession (Ruth 3, Mark 12)
> Gracious God,
>> when we hold back and give only a bit of ourselves,
>>> forgive us;
>> when we let pride and insecurity
>>> keep us from trusting your mercy and grace,
>>>> renew us.
> Have mercy on us,
>> that you might restore our lives
>>> and nourish us as we grow in the love of Christ.
> Strengthen us to give ourselves fully and completely
> to Christ's work in the world. Amen.

Words of Assurance (Ruth 3, Hebrews 9)
> In Christ Jesus, our sins are forgiven
>> and our lives are restored.
> Thanks be to God for this glorious grace!

Passing the Peace of Christ (Ruth 3, Mark 12)
> As we share signs of peace and grace, may we give ourselves fully and completely to one another.

Response to the Word (Ruth 3, Psalm 127, Mark 12)
>One penny or two, one million dollars or two,
>every gift matters to God.
>>**Out of our abundance, out of our poverty,**
>>**we will give fully and completely to Christ.**
>One minute or an hour, one day or a week,
>one year or a lifetime, every moment matters to God.
>>**In our busy schedules, in our slow and lazy days,**
>>**we will give our time fully and completely**
>>**to Christ.**
>As the widow gave her two pennies,
>as Ruth gave her life, as Naomi gave her family,
>we are invited to give ourselves fully and completely,
>that God's realm may be built here on earth.
>*(Worshipers may bring forward pledge and commitment*
>*cards as part of a fall stewardship emphasis, or this response*
>*may flow directly into the morning offering.)*

Thanksgiving and Communion

Invitation to the Offering (Mark 12)
>Bring forth all that you have and all that you are, offering your lives and your love to God.

Offering Prayer (Mark 12)
>As we bring these gifts to you, O God,
>>bless and multiply them,
>>>that those who live in poverty and want
>>>>may find resources and hope.
>Transform our pennies into mission,
>>our dollars into meaning,
>>>and our checks into ministry.
>In Christ's name, we pray. Amen.

Sending Forth

Benediction (Mark 12)

As Jesus gave himself fully and completely,
and as the widow gave all that she had,
may we give ourselves fully and completely
to all whom we meet, and all that God calls us to do.
Go with the love of God!

November 15, 2015

Twenty-fifth Sunday after Pentecost, Proper 28
Laura Jaquith Bartlett

Color

Green

Scripture Readings

1 Samuel 1:4-20; 1 Samuel 2:1-10 (or Psalm 16); Hebrews 10:11-14 (15-18) 19-25; Mark 13:1-8

Theme Ideas

We always want to set up earthly hierarchies, and then worship whatever or whoever is at the top. Even in our churches, we delude ourselves into thinking our buildings themselves are sacred, and somehow the sanctuary is "holier" than the fellowship hall. Jesus assures us that there is nothing sacred about anything as temporary as bricks and mortar. As an infertile woman at the lowest levels of her culture's hierarchy, Hannah was certainly not allowed access to the inner temple, yet God heard and answered her prayers. Hebrews tells us that Jesus himself has given us all access to the true inner temple: the holy heart of God.

Invitation and Gathering

Contemporary Gathering Words (1 Samuel 2)

> *(Have the accompanist/band play "Holy, Holy, Holy," no. 2007 in* The Faith We Sing, *underneath these Gathering Words. Then have the congregation sing the song in either English or Spanish.)*
>
> Come into God's presence in this holy place.
> Feel God's love during this holy time.
> No one on earth is holy like our God—
>> the One who makes the entire world sacred.
> Enter into the holy heart of God.
> *(Congregation sings.)*

Call to Worship (Hebrews 10)

> Come, holy people!
>> **Jesus Christ has made us holy.**
> Come, holy people!
>> **God's Spirit joins us in this holy time.**
> Come, holy people!
>> **God's holy house is open to everyone.**
> Let us worship together!

Opening Prayer (Hebrews 10, 1 Samuel 1)

> Holy God, you have created the world
>> as a holy place.
> Through the life, death, and resurrection
>> of your own Son,
>>> you have transformed each one of us
>>>> into a beloved and sacred being.
> Although we often feel unworthy,
>> Jesus' sacrificial love
>>> gives us the confidence to claim our place
>>>> within your heart.

For embracing our brokenness,
>and for making us whole and holy,
>>we thank you, O God. Amen.

Proclamation and Response

Prayer of Confession (1 Samuel 1, 1 Samuel 2, Hebrews 10, Mark 13)
Dear God, we confess our eagerness
>to create a system of holiness in a world
>>that you have already made holy.
When we make ourselves into guardians of the temple,
>thinking, like Eli, that we know who is worthy
>>and who is not, forgive us.
When we think we know which buildings are holy
>and which are not, forgive us.
Give us eyes to see as you see,
>and grant us the courage to lift up the poor,
>>the hungry, the lowly, and the "unworthy,"
>>>to sit in the seats of honor.
May we be humble enough to truly understand
>that we have been made holy,
>>not through our own actions,
>>>but through the saving love of your Son,
>>>>Jesus Christ. Amen.

Words of Assurance (Hebrews 10:17 NRSV)
God has said, "I will remember their sins
>and their lawless deeds no more."
God's forgiveness wipes our slate clean
>and makes us holy!

Passing the Peace of Christ (Hebrews 10)
Greet each person around you with these words:
You are a holy child of God!

Response to the Word (Hebrews 10)
> God, you have written your law, your name,
>> and your image onto our hearts.
> Through the sacrifice of your Son,
>> you have made us holy.
> All your world is holy, O God.
> No part of this earth is more sacred than any other.
> Empower us with your Spirit
>> to live in holy peace
>>> with all our sisters and brothers. Amen.

Thanksgiving and Communion

Invitation to the Offering (Hebrews 10, Mark 13)
> Look around you! These stones, this plaster, these walls, this entire structure…we do not give our money, or our lives, just to support buildings. No, our money, our lives, and even our buildings are all focused on the ministry of the One who makes them holy. Out of holy abundance, let us offer our gifts. Out of holy obedience, let us offer our lives.

Offering Prayer (1 Samuel 2, Hebrews 10)
> God, keep us from the temptation
>> of thinking that we have made ourselves holy
>>> by supporting your church
>>>> through these offerings.
> Remind us once more,
>> that there is no admission fee
>>> to gain entrance into your heart.
> Accept these gifts, therefore,
>> as our commitment to bring about your vision
>>> of hungry people fed, and needy people satisfied.

255

As we work to serve our brothers and sisters,
we celebrate and exalt your holy name. Amen.

Sending Forth

Benediction (Hebrews 10)
Go out from this holy place into the holy world,
knowing that you are held close in God's heart.
Holy are you, O God!
Go out from this holy place into the holy world,
knowing that Christ has entered into your brokenness
and has made you whole.
Holy are you, O Christ!
Go out from this holy place into the holy world,
knowing that the Spirit will keep your hope
unwavering.
Holy are you, O Spirit!
Go in peace as holy people. Amen.

November 22, 2015

Christ the King/Reign of Christ Sunday
B. J. Beu

[Copyright © 2014 by B. J. Beu. Used by permission.]

Color

White

Scripture Readings

2 Samuel 23:1-7; Psalm 132:1-12; Revelation 1:4b-8; John 18:33-37

Theme Ideas

Kingship, both human and divine, focuses today's readings. Though a flawed vessel, King David is portrayed as an ideal king and ruler. The conclusion of 2 Samuel is an oracle, spoken through the mouth of King David, proclaiming the commitment of his house and lineage to God's everlasting covenant. David trusted the Lord. In Psalm 132, David forswears sleep until a resting place is found for the ark of God. Yet, even David's piety, and God's promise of an everlasting covenant, cannot keep David's line from falling into sin. Divine kingship alone is faithful. Revelation 1 and John 18 herald this kingship. Those who are entrenched in this world cannot see it, but everyone who belongs to the truth listens to the voice of Christ, their king. Ultimately, all human rulers fail us. Christ alone is our rightful king and sovereign.

Invitation and Gathering

Contemporary Gathering Words (Revelation 21, John 18)
Our leaders disappoint and fail us.
Follow Christ, ruler of the kings of the earth.
Deceitful words are ever in our ears.
Belong to the truth, and listen to Christ's voice.
Charlatans seek our allegiance.
Hold fast to Christ, our Lord and King.

Call to Worship (2 Samuel 23, Psalm 132, John 18)
Christ has come to be our king.
We have come to be Christ's people.
Clothed in righteousness, Christ has come to save us.
Let the faithful shout for joy.
Like the sun rising on a cloudless morning,
Christ disperses the darkness with justice and mercy.
Worship the prince of peace.

Opening Prayer (2 Samuel 23, Revelation 1)
Strong One of Israel,
    with grace and peace,
        you clothe your people
            in the garments of salvation.
Open our eyes,
    that we may behold your glory,
        and witness your Son
            coming with the clouds,
                to rule with justice and righteousness.

Open our ears,
>that we may hear his voice
>>calling us to shine like dew on the grass.
Open our hearts,
>that we may love as he loves,
>>and live as he lives. Amen.

Proclamation and Response

Prayer of Confession (2 Samuel 23, Revelation 1, John 18)
Rock of Israel,
>you are the bedrock of our lives,
>>the foundation of our hopes and dreams,
>>>yet we seldom trust or rely on your strength.
We have stopped looking up to see your appearance
>coming in the clouds.
Instead, we have all turned to our own devices,
>only to discover that our lives are built upon sand.
Forgive us, Lord.
Help us affix our gaze on Christ's kingdom,
>that our future might be built on a solid foundation
>>with Christ as our king and cornerstone. Amen.

Assurance of Pardon (Psalm 132)
God made a covenant with King David,
>promising faithfulness to his descendants.
In Christ, God has made a new covenant with us,
>promising forgiveness of sins and fullness of grace.
Thanks be to God!

Passing the Peace of Christ (Revelation 1)
Grace and peace to you from the One who is, who was, and who is to come. Grace and peace to you from the

One who shines in our lives like the sun rising on a cloudless morning. Shining with God's joy, let us share signs of the peace of Christ, our Lord and King.

Introduction to the Word (2 Samuel 23)

The Spirit of the Lord speaks to us,
teaching us lessons that endure.
The King of kings calls to us,
beckoning us to follow.
The Light of light shines on us,
illuminating the mind of the wise.
The Spirit of the Lord speaks to us,
leading us into life.
Listen for the word of God.

Response to the Word (John 18:37b-38 NRSV)

Jesus said: "For this I was born, and for this I came into the world, to testify to the truth. Everyone who belongs to the truth listens to my voice." To which Pilate responded: "What is truth?" As people of faith, do we follow Pilate or do we follow Jesus? Are we sophisticated men and women who understand that truth is relative, that the things we believe in are only true from a certain perspective? Or are we willing to accept that a deeper truth claims our allegiance, even if we struggle to grasp it? How we answer this question makes all the difference in the world.

Thanksgiving and Communion

Invitation to the Offering (Revelation 1)

The Alpha and Omega, the first and the last, the One who was and is and is to come, is the Lord God Almighty. Let us glorify the One who offers us every blessing as we share our tithes and offerings.

Offering Prayer (2 Samuel 23, Psalm 132)
Strong One of Israel,
    open our eyes to your splendor:
        the light sparkling on the waters;
        the sun dawning on a new day;
        the dew on the grass;
        the glistening promise of fresh possibilities
            in our lives each morning.
For you bless the people with provisions;
    you bless the poor with bread.
Receive the gifts of our hands,
    that through these offerings,
        all may come to know your bounty,
            with Christ as their king. Amen.

Sending Forth

Benediction (2 Samuel 23, Psalm 132, Revelation 1)
The Mighty One of Jacob clothes us with righteousness.
    We go with God's blessing.
The Rock of Israel brings us joy.
    We go with Christ's blessing.
The Alpha and Omega sends us forth.
    We go with the Spirit's blessing.

—Or—

Benediction (2 Samuel 23, Revelation 1, John 18)
God is faithful.
    God's promises are sure.
Christ is righteous and just.
    Christ's kingdom never ends.
The Spirit is with us always.
    The Spirit's love leads us home.

November 26, 2015

Thanksgiving Day
Mary J. Scifres

Color

Red or White

Scripture Readings

Joel 2:21-27; Psalm 126; 1 Timothy 2:1-7; Matthew 6:25-33

Theme Ideas

Rejoice and give thanks! This is a day to remember the gifts and blessings that God showers in our lives. This is a season to trust God's providential care and to rest assured that we are held in Christ's gentle arms of love. In a world that instills fear and worry that nothing we have will ever be enough, we discover in Christ's arms that we have everything we need.

Invitation and Gathering

Contemporary Gathering Words (Psalm 126, Matthew 6)
When God restored the fortunes of Zion,
the Israelites wandered home as if in a dream.

Let us be a people who wander in our dreams.
Wander amongst God's marvelous creation!
Wonder at the amazing things God has done!
Do not worry about your life, today or tomorrow.
Trust that God values us even more greatly
    than birds and flowers,
    no matter how beautiful they may be.
Know that God treasures us completely,
    and gives us all that we will ever need.

Call to Worship (Joel 2, Psalm 126)

Come with hearts overflowing in gratitude.
God has done great things for us.
Be glad and rejoice.
We rejoice in God's gifts.
Sing praises of joy.
Our mouths are filled with laughter.
Shout with thanksgiving, in sunshine and rain.
Praise God for our lives, for harvest and food.

Opening Prayer (Joel 2, Matthew 6)

Giver of life,
    for sunshine and showers,
      we give you thanks;
    for food and drink,
      we give you praise;
    for clothing and shelter,
      we bestow our gratitude.
Gather our worries and our burdens this day,
    and shelter us from fear and despair.
Help us rest assured in your arms,
    knowing that your loving care is enough.
It is enough.
It is enough. Amen.

Proclamation and Response

Prayer of Confession (Psalm 126, Matthew 6)
God of abundant love,
    sprinkle the tears we have sown
        with your mercy and hope,
            that we may reap a harvest of joy;
    replace our selfish dreams of wealth and prestige,
        with gratitude for what we have,
            that we may find contentment in life.
Turn our dreams to you, O Lord,
    and remind us of the abundance you offer,
        for you have done great things for us,
            turning our tears into shouts of joy.

Words of Assurance (Psalm 126, Matthew 6)
Through Christ, God's love has done great things for us.
Through Christ, God's grace restores our life
    and makes us whole once more.

Passing the Peace of Christ (1 Timothy 2, Matthew 6)
Share with one another signs of peace and love. Show
Christ to one another, that we may be reminded of the
peace that passes all understanding.

Response to the Word
Remember this day the gifts and blessings that God
showers in our lives. This is a season to trust God's
providential care and to rest assured that we are held
in Christ's gentle arms of love. In those arms, we have
everything we need. Rejoice and give thanks!

Thanksgiving and Communion

Invitation to the Offering (Joel 2)

Be glad and rejoice! Just as summer brought green forests and sunny days, so now fall brings abundant fields and changing leaves. As the rain falls upon us, may we remember that the seasons, the fertile earth, and the blessings they yield, are gifts from God to be shared with those in need.

Offering Prayer

Bountiful God,
> we look forward to your harvest each year.

Our tables overflow
> with the goodness of your green earth,
>> but our tables pale in comparison
>>> to the splendor that awaits us,
>>>> and all of your children,
>>>>> at your heavenly banquet.

Receive these offerings,
> as we thank you for your many blessings.

Help us be mindful of those who go without,
> as we feast and make merry
>> during this festive season. Amen.

(B. J. Beu)

Call to Prayer (1 Timothy 2)

I urge you, sisters and brothers, to bring your supplications, prayers, intercessions, and thanksgiving to God.

Prayer of Thanksgiving and Intercession (Joel 2, 1 Timothy 2, Matthew 6)

Giver of life,
> we bless you for your many gifts—

the gifts of sunshine and rain,
the gifts of summer and fall.
For the coming winter and the change of seasons,
we give you thanks.
For the blessings of our lives
and the opportunities to experience joy,
we give you praise.
Even as we thank you and return these gifts to you,
we remember that many are in need
of your love and care.
Help us worry more for others
than we do for ourselves.
Be with those who struggle for daily needs.
Empower those who live in fear and violence.
Encourage those who suffer in sorrow and despair.
Restore our fortunes, O Lord—
not the fortunes of money and power,
but the fortunes of love and mercy,
the gifts of grace and peace.
Strengthen us as we strive for your kingdom
and your righteousness in our lives,
through Christ, our Lord. Amen.

Sending Forth

Benediction (Psalm 126, Matthew 6)
Go forth with shouts of joy.
Proclaim the greatness of God!
Be glad and rejoice in Christ's care.
Trust the promises of God!

November 29, 2015

First Sunday of Advent

Joanne Carlson Brown

Color

Purple

Scripture Readings

Jeremiah 33:14-16; Psalm 25:1-10; 1 Thessalonians 3:9-13; Luke 21:25-36

Theme Ideas

Sometimes the first Sunday of Advent feels like Chicken Little: The sky is falling! The sky is falling! The Gospel's apocalyptic signs and portents make for a surprising and gloomy start to what is such a joyous time. But it is a time of waiting and looking—a time of being alert and believing in the fulfillment of prophecy. The One promised is coming. Watch out!

Invitation and Gathering

Contemporary Gathering Words (Luke 21)

One: Did you see the moon last night?
Two: Yeah, and how about the stars?

One:	I hear the sea is really going crazy.
Two:	*What do you think it all means?*
One:	It could be the end of the world.
Two:	*Or maybe just the end as we know it.*
One:	I read once it's a sign that someone's coming.
Two:	*Yeah, the Promised One.*
All:	**Be alert and watch out, now and always.**

Call to Worship (Jeremiah 33, Luke 21)

The days are coming when God will fulfill the promise
made to our ancestors.
> **A righteous branch of David's lineage
> shall come forth.**
There will be justice and righteousness in the land.
> **This is our salvation.**
Let us worship the God of promises and signs.
with eyes to see the signs of God's promises.

Opening Prayer (Psalm 25, Luke 21)

O God, the times and signs are confusing.
During this time of worship,
> help us know your ways,
> > and see clearly
> > > the coming of the Promised One.
Lead us in your truth and teach us.
For we wait with hopeful expectation:
> to see; to know; to believe.
To you we lift our souls in trust and love,
> knowing you will hold them
> > in your loving hands. Amen.

Proclamation and Response

Prayer of Confession (Luke 21)

God of promise,
today's Gospel reads like the end of the world,
and we don't know what to make of it.
We read of fig leaves sprouting, portents in the sky,
and people not passing away
until Jesus' words have come to pass.
After 2000 years of waiting for the end to come,
It's hard to drum up much expectation.
We go our way as if nothing is happening,
expecting nothing and no one.
Break into our complacency with your word.
Help us to raise our heads, look up, and be alert.
Help us believe and live in full expectation
that something is happening in our world,
that you are breaking into our world
and into our lives.
Forgive us when we miss your coming
because we are looking in the wrong places.
Help us perceive that the beloved community is near.
Amen.

Words of Assurance (Psalm 25, Jeremiah 33)

For those who come to God in humble contrition
and seek to live the covenant of God's ways,
the paths of God are steadfast love and faithfulness.
Know that you are in the hands of a God
who loves you fiercely and steadfastly.
Trust in the promises of God.

Passing the Peace of Christ (Jeremiah 33, Luke 21)

Turn to those around you and greet them with the words: The Promised One is coming!

Introduction to the Word (Jeremiah 33, Luke 21)

May our ears and hearts be open to words of signs and portents, words of promises fulfilled. May they touch our souls and help us be alert to all that God is doing around us.

Response to the Word (Psalm 25, Jeremiah 33, Luke 21)

For words of life;
for words of promise;
for words of salvation,
we give God thanks and praise.

Thanksgiving and Communion

Invitation to the Offering (Jeremiah 33, Luke 21)

We have been told the days are surely coming. We have been given signs. The Promised One is coming. And we wait in expectation. We have a message to give the world—a message of promises about to be fulfilled. Our offering will enable this church community to proclaim this message as clearly as we can. It also enables us individually to show our gratitude, even as we wait. Our morning offering will now be received.

Offering Prayer (Psalm 25, Jeremiah 33, Luke 21)

We dedicate our resources and our very selves
to the One who fulfills promises,
who holds us in steadfast love,

and who calls us to be alert, to watch out,
to be ready.
For that we are truly grateful.

Sending Forth

Benediction (Psalm 25, Jeremiah 33, Luke 21)
Be alert, watch, be ready.
We will wait for the Promised One to arrive.
Go now from this fellowship:
knowing that you are following the ways of God;
knowing that you are actively waiting
for the Promised One, who is with you always;
knowing that the Spirit will guide you
until all is fulfilled.
**We will wait for the Promised One
to lead us home.**

December 6, 2015

Second Sunday of Advent
B. J. Beu

[Copyright © 2014 by B. J. Beu. Used by permission.]

Color

Purple

Scripture Readings

Malachi 3:1-4; Luke 1:68-79; Philippians 1:3-11; Luke 3:1-6

Theme Ideas

The message of God's salvation is like a refiner's fire or fullers' soap, cleansing us of our impurities. While the advent of the Messiah is marked with hopeful expectation, preparing for that arrival places demands upon our lives. With words that confront our complacency, John the Baptist warns us to repent and amend our ways. Christ is coming—bringing hope, eagerness, and anticipation, but also a little fear and trepidation—like a refiner's fire and fuller's soap.

Invitation and Gathering

Contemporary Gathering Words (Luke 1, Luke 3)
A voice cries out in the wilderness:
    "Prepare the way of the Lord!"

A challenge is uttered from on high:
   "Make God's paths straight."
For every valley will be lifted up,
and every mountain will be made low.
      Every crooked path will be made straight,
      and every rough way will be made smooth.
All will see the salvation of our God.

Call to Worship (Luke 3)
   How shall we prepare for the coming of the Lord?
      With hearts filled with love and peace.
   How shall we prepare for the coming of Christ?
      With prayers filled with adoration and devotion.
   How shall we prepare for the coming of our savior?
      With songs filled with joy and hope.
   How shall we prepare for the coming of the Son of God?
      With worship filled with passion and spirit.
   Come! Let us worship.

Opening Prayer (Luke 1, Philippians 1, Luke 3)
   God of love and renewal,
         enter the wilderness of our lives,
            and call us to prepare once more
               for the coming of your Son.
   Fill the valleys of our insecurities with hope,
      and bring low the mountains
         of our pride and conceit.
   Make straight the paths before us,
      and guide our feet in the ways of peace. Amen.

Proclamation and Response

Prayer of Confession (Malachi 3, Luke 1, Luke 3)
   Holy One, by the tender mercy of your grace,
      you shine the light of your love

into the shadow of our lives,
>that those who sit in darkness
>>may find peace and hope.
Shine your light on us, O God,
>for we have heard your call
>>to prepare the way of the Lord,
>>>yet we feel the vestiges of death
>>>>cling to us like a bitter frost.
Come to us like a refiner's fire and fullers' soap,
>that we may be purified in body and soul
>>and made ready to make your paths straight,
>>>that all may see your salvation. Amen.

Assurance of Pardon (Luke 1)

In Christ, God brings light to our darkness,
>and life to all who sit in the shadow of death.
In Christ, all who seek the Lord find life anew.

Introduction to the Word (Philippians 1)

The One who began a good work in us will bring it to conclusion. The One who leads us into holiness and righteousness speaks to us still. Listen for the word of God.

Response to the Word or Benediction (Malachi 3, Luke 1, Luke 3)

Like a refiner's fire and fullers' soap,
>**God polishes our lives**
>**brighter than the finest silver.**
Like the dawning of a new day,
>**God breaks into our darkness,**
>**and fills us with light, love, and joy.**
Like a merciful judge,
>**God offers us repentance,**
>**and guides our feet in the ways of peace.**

Thanksgiving and Communion

Invitation to the Offering *(Malachi 3, Luke 3)*

Prepare the way of the Lord. Prepare with open hearts and hands ready to share. Prepare with gifts of love and mercy. Come, let us prepare the way of the Lord with offerings pleasing to our God.

Offering Prayer *(Malachi 3, Luke 1)*

Blessed redeemer,
    as you rescued your people of old,
        so you rescue us over and over again.
Like a refiner's fire and fullers' soap,
    you have purified our lives
        like works of fine silver and gold.
From the brightness of your dawn,
    we bring our offering to you this day,
        that those who sit in darkness,
            may find in these gifts
                light and hope,
                    compassion and love. Amen.

Sending Forth

Benediction *(Luke 1, Luke 3)*

God meets us in the wilderness of our lives,
preparing our hearts to meet the Lord.
    Christ guides our feet in the ways of life.
God fills the valleys of our hearts
and brings low the mountains of our pride.
    Christ guides our feet in the ways of love.
God makes straight the paths of our feet
and smoothes out the rough edges of our journey.

Christ guides our feet in the ways of peace.
Go and prepare the way of the Lord.

—Or—

Benediction (Philippians 1)
May your love overflow in mercy and compassion,
    as you walk pure and blameless
    in the ways of Christ.
May you produce a harvest of righteousness
    as you grow in faith as Christ's disciples,
    to the glory and praise of God.

December 13, 2015

Third Sunday of Advent
B. J. Beu

Color

Purple

Scripture Readings

Zephaniah 3:14-20; Isaiah 12:2-6; Philippians 4:4-7; Luke 3:7-18

Theme Ideas

With the exception of the Gospel lesson, Philippians captures the mood of the day: "Rejoice in the Lord always; again I say, Rejoice" (v. 4 NRSV). God's salvation is at hand. Isaiah and Zephaniah invite us to sing aloud and shout for joy. Through God, the warrior receives victory, while the lame and outcast no longer live in shame. While three of today's lections celebrate the joy of our salvation, the Gospel lesson reminds us that salvation demands more than our joy, it calls for repentance as well. John the Baptizer warns of God's wrath for those who hear the good news yet reject it. Salvation requires justice; it also entails judgment, and we need to be ready. Yet, in all this, we are called to rejoice.

Invitation and Gathering

Contemporary Gathering Words or Benediction (Zephaniah 3, Isaiah 12)

Shout to the Lord, you sons of God.

Sing aloud, you daughters of the living God.

Salvation has drawn near.

Shout for joy, you sons of the Lord.

Sing your praises, you daughters of the Most High.

Salvation is at hand.

Call to Worship (Zephaniah 3, Isaiah 12, Philippians 4:4)

Rejoice in the Lord always, again I say rejoice!

With joyful hearts, we draw living water

from the wellspring of God's salvation.

With loud singing, we return to a home of love.

With loud shouts, we return to our God.

Rejoice in the Lord always, again I say rejoice!

Opening Prayer (Zephaniah 3, Isaiah 12)

Redeemer God,

with laughter in our mouths

and joy in our hearts,

we draw living water

from the wellspring of your salvation.

For you save the lame

and gather the outcast,

turning their shame into praise.

You gather the lost

and bring the exile home at last.

Who is like you in all the earth?

There are none that compare to you, O God.

In your presence, we dwell secure.

In your love, we find the power
to transform the world. Amen.

Proclamation and Response

Prayer of Confession (Luke 3)
Author of everlasting life,
we are quick to claim
the joys and blessings of our baptism,
but we are quick to forget
the cost of Christian discipleship;
we are eager to draw from the wellspring
of your salvation,
but shrink from the refining fire
of your baptism.
Remind us once more, O God,
that your good news carries more than the hope
of your blessing for our lives,
it carries the expectation
that we will amend our ways.
It is not enough to praise you with our lips,
we must also love you with our actions:
by sharing our wealth,
by showing mercy to the needy,
and by protecting the weak and defenseless.
In these things are you praised.
In these things do we show our faith and fidelity.
Heal our hearts, compassionate One,
that we may be a people of true repentance—
a people who prepare for your Son's birth
by embracing the ones he loved. Amen.

Words of Assurance (Zephaniah 3, Luke 3)
>Although the axe is lying at the root of the tree,
>>do not despair.
>When we return to God with full and honest hearts,
>>Christ takes away the judgments against us,
>>and brings us the joy of our salvation.

Introduction to the Word (Zephaniah 3)
>The Lord is in our midst. Let all who wish to know the ways of life and death, listen for the word of God.

Response to the Word (Isaiah 12)
>Give thanks to the Lord.
>Call on God's holy name.
>Make known God's deeds among the peoples.
>Sing praises to God,
>>for great in our midst is the Holy One of Israel.

Thanksgiving and Communion

Offering Prayer (Zephaniah 3)
>God of our salvation,
>>with a strong hand and mighty arm
>>>you save us from our foes
>>>>and rejoice over us with gladness.
>How can we repay you for your love and grace?
>Receive our thanks and humble appreciation
>>for all that you have given us
>>>which makes us what we are.
>Bless these gifts and offerings,
>>that they may bring peace and hope
>>>to your people in need. Amen.

Sending Forth

Benediction (Philippians 4)

Rejoice! The Lord is near.
Take heart and do not worry about your life,
    for it is God's pleasure to give you the kingdom.
May the peace of God that passes all understanding,
    guard your hearts and minds in Christ Jesus.

December 20, 2015

Fourth Sunday of Advent

Mary J. Scifres

Color

Purple

Scripture Readings

Micah 5:2-5a; Luke 1:46b-55; Hebrews 10:5-10;
Luke 1:39-45

Theme Ideas

On this fourth Sunday of Advent, like Mary, we are
pregnant with expectation. Something amazing is coming on Christmas day, and we can hardly wait. Even if
we don't feel this way as Christmas approaches, today's
scriptures call us to joyous expectation. When Micah
prophesies to Bethlehem, he proclaims a joyous hope
for one who will come forth to bring security and peace,
and nurture and strength, to the entire nation. When
Elizabeth receives Mary's visit with joyous expectation,
she is filled with the Holy Spirit. When Mary receives
Elizabeth's blessing, she is filled with a new hope and
confidence for the blessing she carries for the world. As

Christmas approaches, remember to be pregnant with expectation. Only then may we notice the amazing miracle of Christmas anew; only then may we receive the blessings of Christ's presence with joy and hope.

Invitation and Gathering

Contemporary Gathering Words (Luke 1)
Traveling to the hill country,
Mary visited her cousin Elizabeth.
Journeys can change our lives.
Traveling to meet Mary,
Elizabeth was filled with the Holy Spirit.
Journeys can change our lives.
Traveling together, they discovered they were pregnant,
not just with two boys, but with expectation and hope.
Journeys can change our lives.
May this journey of worshiping together
bring us the same hopeful expectation
as we journey with God this day.

Call to Worship (Luke 1)
God has done great things for us.
Glory to God in the highest!
God is doing great things for us.
Glory to God in the highest!
God will do great things for us.
Glory to God in the highest!

Opening Prayer (Luke 1)
God of expectation, fill us with hope this day.
Birth in us an expectation of goodness and grace.
Pour out your Holy Spirit upon us,

that we may perceive your presence in the world,
and jump for joy at the blessings and hope
all around us.

Proclamation and Response

Prayer of Confession (Luke 1)
We wait, Gracious God,
but seldom do so patiently,
much less with joyous anticipation.
Forgive us when we expect the worst.
Forgive us when we are pregnant with bitterness.
Forgive us when we give birth to anger and hatred,
rather than kindness and love.
Restore us with the gift of your grace,
and fill us with the power of your Holy Spirit:
that we may be pregnant with expectation;
that we may give birth to hope and joy;
that we may grow into a people
of peace and love.
In Christ's name, we pray. Amen.

Words of Assurance (Luke 1)
Rise in joy and hope,
for God will lift you up when you are downtrodden,
and fill you with good things when you are hungry.
Rise in joy and hope,
for God's mercy is true, and in Christ
we are forgiven and redeemed.

Passing the Peace of Christ (Micah 5, Luke 1)
Christ came to bring us peace. As we share signs of love
and peace with one another, let us be Christ's people of
peace.

Introduction to the Word (Luke 1)

Mary was pregnant with Jesus. Elizabeth was pregnant with John. Both were pregnant with expectation for God's magnificent blessings and miracles. As we hear their stories, let us listen with expectation and hope.

Response to the Word (Luke 1)

God looks with favor on the lowest of the low, and the hungriest of the poor. Where might we need God's favor to lift us from despair and to restore our hopeful expectation? I invite you to reflect and pray silently for the places in your lives where you need God's nourishment and strength. *(Allow time for silent prayer or for people to write their needs down to be brought forward during the offering.)*

God looks with favor on the lowest of the low, and the hungriest of the poor. Where might you need to offer God's favor to lift someone from despair or to restore their hopeful expectation? I invite you to reflect and pray silently for the places in your lives where others need God's nourishment and strength. *(Allow time for silent prayer or for people to write their prayers and commitments down to be brought forward during the offering.)*

—Or—

Response to the Word (Luke 1)

Blessed be the God of Israel,
> who helps us and delivers God's people,
> by raising up for us a mighty savior in Christ Jesus,
> and by restoring our hope of receiving
>> God's goodness
> all the days of our lives.
> **Glory to God in the highest!**

Thanksgiving and Communion

Invitation to the Offering (Luke 1)
> Let us glorify God with the gifts we now give, that others may know the glorious hope of Christ Jesus.

Offering Prayer (Luke 1)
> Glorious God, bless these gifts,
>> that they may lift up the lowly,
>>> fill the hungry with good things,
>>>> and give strength and mercy
>>>>> to those most in need.
> In your holy name, we pray. Amen.

The Great Thanksgiving (Luke 1)
> The Lord be with you.
>> **And also with you.**
> Lift up your hearts.
>> **We lift them up to the Lord.**
> Let us give thanks to the Lord our God.
>> **It is right to give our thanks and praise.**

> It is right, and a good and joyful thing,
>> always and everywhere to give thanks to you,
>> to glorify and rejoice in your presence,
>> almighty God, creator of heaven and earth.
> In ancient days, you created us in your image
>> and lifted us up to be your people.
> When we turned away and chose despair over hope,
>> you remained steadfast and blessed us,
>> giving us the opportunity to bear life,
>> that we might give birth to expectation and hope.
> Even when we fell short of your glorious hope,

you lifted us up from the depths of despair
and freed us from the bondage of hopelessness.
And in the fullness of time, you sent your Son,
Jesus Christ, to free us from the bondage of slavery
to sin and death,
And so, with your people on earth,
and all the company of heaven,
we praise your name
and join their unending hymn, saying:
Holy, holy, holy Lord, God of power and might,
heaven and earth are full of your glory.
Hosanna in the highest. Blessed is the one
who comes in the name of the Lord.
Hosanna in the highest.

Holy are you and blessed is the fruit of Mary's womb,
your Son Jesus Christ.
When you sent Jesus to this earth,
you filled us with a new hope,
calling us to be pregnant with expectation
and giving birth to love and peace in your world.
Through Christ's constant love and never-ending grace,
we are invited into your presence,
lifted up from our lowliness,
given mercy and strength,
rescued from our sins,
and filled with your goodness and grace.

And so we come to your table,
to be fed with your grace,
as we remember the story of our faith.
On the night before his death, Jesus took bread,

gave thanks to you, broke the bread,
gave it to the disciples, and said,
"Take, eat; this is my body which is given for you.
Do this in remembrance of me."
When the supper was over, Jesus took the cup,
gave thanks to you, gave it to the disciples, and said,
"Drink from this, all of you; this is my life
in the new covenant,
poured out for you and for many
for the forgiveness of sins.
Do this, as often as you drink it,
in remembrance of me."

And so, in remembrance of these
your mighty acts of love and grace,
we offer ourselves in praise and thanksgiving,
as children of your covenant
in union with Christ's love for us,
as we proclaim the mystery of faith.
Christ has died.
Christ is risen.
Christ will come again.

Communion Prayer (Luke 1)
Pour out your Holy Spirit
on all of us gathered here,
and on these gifts of bread and wine.
Fill us with the good things of your eternal presence,
that we might be your presence in the world.
By your Spirit, make us one with Christ,
one with each other,
and one in ministry to all the world,
until Christ comes in final victory
and we feast at your heavenly banquet.

Through Jesus Christ,
>with the Holy Spirit in your holy Church,
>>all honor and glory are yours, almighty God,
>>>now and forevermore. Amen.

Giving the Bread and Cup
(The bread and wine are given to the people with these or other words of blessing.)
The life of Christ, living in you.
The love of Christ, flowing through you.

Sending Forth

Benediction (Luke 1)
Blessed are you when you carry Christ's hope
to the world.
>**Blessed are we when we carry Christ's hope to the world.**
Pregnant with expectation,
waiting with hope and joy,
>**We go forth to bless the world!**

December 24, 2015

Christmas Eve
Safiyah Fosua

Color

White

Scripture Readings

Isaiah 9:2-7; Psalm 96; Titus 2:11-14; Luke 2:1-20

Theme Ideas

We never tire of the Christmas story or its notes of wonder
and awe. Isaiah and Luke remind us that Christ came for
us—*all of us*. In this season of giving and gifting, how will
we receive the news of the greatest gift ever offered to us?

Invitation and Gathering

Contemporary Gathering Words (Luke 2)
Joy to the world! Christ has come.
He did not come riding on a war horse from the clouds.
He came to us vulnerable and defenseless,
    born to a poor young couple
    with no place to lay him down but a manger!
God's Son was not sent to go to war against us
    over our wickedness.

He came to instruct us,
>to make peace between us and God,
>and to heal us—*all of us.*
Joy to the world! Christ has come!

Call to Worship (Isaiah 9:6b, Luke 2)
Glory to God for the gift of a Son.
>**Glory to God for Jesus.**
Glory to God for sending a Son.
>**Glory to God for Jesus:**
>**Wonderful Counselor, Mighty God,**
>**Everlasting Father, Prince of Peace!**
Glory to God for the gift of a Son.
>**Glory to God for Jesus!**

Opening Prayer (Luke 2)
God, we gather tonight,
>in breathless wonder and awe,
>>to remember the birth of Jesus.
The very God, very man,
>real-life, on our level, gift of your Son
>>is a gift greater than we could ever earn
>>>or deserve.
Thank you, Lord,
>for leaving the splendor of heaven
>>to dwell with us for a season. Amen.

—Or—

Opening Prayer
O wondrous God of the stars,
>we come tonight with breathless wonder,
>>to see the babe who will change our lives.
We hear the names Wonderful Counselor,
>Mighty God, Prince of Peace,
>>and we are in awe.

You have touched the earth this night
    with your unconditional love.
Touch our hearts and minds and souls—
    that we may never tire of this story,
        or take it for granted.
Make this night magical again. Amen.
(Joanne Carlson Brown)

Proclamation and Response

Prayer of Confession (Isaiah 9, Luke 2)
Prepare our hearts, O God,
    to receive the Christ Child once more.
When we are lost in darkness,
    shine your light
        into the darkness of our world.
When the gloom clings tightly to us,
    shine your glory
        into the shadows of our lives.
Overcome our fear, Holy One,
    and inspire us to leave our flocks,
        and seek the Christ Child this night.
Prepare our hearts, O God,
    to behold your precious gift
        in awe and wonder.
(B. J. Beu)

Words of Assurance (Isaiah 9:2 NRSV)
"The people who walked in darkness
have seen a great light;
    those who lived in a land of deep darkness—
    on them light has shined."
Receive forgiveness. Receive light.
Walk in God's light. Forgiven.

Passing the Peace of Christ

On this holy night of incarnate love, let us share signs of the peace that came down to earth to bring us joy.
(B. J. Beu)

Response to the Word (Luke 2)

Glory to God!
Glory to God in the highest!
Glory to God in the highest heaven!
Glory to God for the gift of Jesus' birth!

Thanksgiving and Communion

Invitation to the Offering

Come now and kneel before the Christ Child. Bring all that you are and all that you have. Offer your gifts in wonder and surprise, awe and reverence. Offer your gifts in joy and delight.
(Joanne Carlson Brown)

Offering Prayer (Luke 2)

Gracious God, in this season of gift-giving,
   we come to offer our gifts to you,
      knowing that we can never repay you
         for the gift of your Son. Amen.

Sending Forth

Benediction (Luke 2)

At a time when hope was most needed,
God sent Jesus into the world to instruct us,
to make peace between us and God,
and to heal us.

Christ, our Savior has come, and will come again!
Go from this place to spread the good news

—Or—

Benediction
Go in wonder.
Go to bring light to those who sit in darkness,
    joy to those who have tasted bitter tears,
    and magic to a world bereft of hope.
Go with the songs of angels in your ears,
    and the love of God in your hearts.
Go and spread the word
    that Christ the Lord is born this night.
(Joanne Carlson Brown and B. J. Beu)

December 27, 2015

First Sunday after Christmas
Mary J. Scifres

[Copyright © 2014 by Mary J. Scifres. Used by permission.]

Color

White

Scripture Readings

1 Samuel 2:18-20, 26; Psalm 148; Colossians 3:12-17; Luke 2:41-52

Theme Ideas

Doing everything in the name of God is a high calling, and yet the entire membership of the Colossian church is called to do just that (Colossians 3:17). This is the calling and commitment that Hannah answered in dedicating Samuel to the temple, who in turn dedicated his entire life to God. By being in his "Father's house" as a young boy, Jesus was dedicating his life, words, and actions to God—even when it stressed out his parents. The psalmist calls every part of creation to proclaim God's praise. We are called and challenged to dedicate all that we do, and all that we say, in the name of Jesus, to the glory of God. This is a high calling indeed.

Invitation and Gathering

Contemporary Gathering Words (Psalm 148, Colossians 3)
Holy, loved children of God, put on compassion
and kindness this day.
Wrapped in the garment of love,
we gather to worship God.
Holy, loved children of God, with humility
clothe yourselves in gentleness, and patience.
Wrapped in the garment of love,
we gather as the family of God.
Holy, loved children of God, bring your gratitude
and your joy to worship.
Wrapped in the garment of love,
we gather to sing praise to God.

Call to Worship (Psalm 148, Colossians 3)
Listen for God's word this day.
May the word of Christ live richly within us.
Give thanks for God's good gifts.
We will sing hymns and songs of praise.
Rejoice and be glad in Christ, our savior.
We will worship Christ in spirit and in truth.

Opening Prayer (Colossians 3)
Nourish us, holy and loving God,
that we may grow in wisdom
as Samuel and Jesus before us.
Clothe us with compassion and kindness,
that we may grow in love and unity,
through the power of your Holy Spirit,
in whose name we pray. Amen.

—*Or*—

Opening Prayer (Colossians 3, Luke 2)
> God of wisdom and grace,
>> may your Spirit grow within us,
>>> that we may grow in wisdom and truth
>>>> all the days of our lives.
> Teach us your ways,
>> that we may walk the path of Christ
>>> and lead others into your light.
> Clothe us, gracious God,
>> with compassion and kindness,
>> with humility and gentleness,
>>> that others may see in us
>>>> the truth of your love.
> Bind us together in love and unity,
>> that our church may be a haven of blessing
>>> and a place of peace. Amen.

Proclamation and Response

Prayer of Confession (Colossians 3)
> You have chosen us for yourself, O God,
>> and yet we choose other paths,
>>> other roads, other priorities.
> Guide us back to you.
> Forgive us, gracious One:
>> when we destroy harmony;
>> when we wear anger like a cloak;
>> when we weave discontent and malice
>>> into the fabric of our lives;
>> when we withhold forgiveness from one another.
> Clothe us with your love and mercy,
>> that we may live as your people
>>> and put on love and mercy.

Dwell in us once more,
    that we may live as people of compassion,
        kindness, humility, and patience.
Bind us together with your powerful love,
    that our love may be pure,
        and our actions may reflect the peace of Christ
            calling us into unity and harmony.

Words of Assurance (Colossians 3)
Be thankful in this good news:
    Christ has forgiven us.
    Christ is forgiving us.
    Christ will forgive us.
In the name of Christ Jesus, we are forgiven
    and clothed in love!

Passing the Peace of Christ (Colossians 3)
The peace of Christ calls us into one body, one church,
one family of God. Proclaim this good news as you share
signs of peace and love.

Introduction to the Word (Colossians 3)
Listen, that the word of Christ may live richly in you—
in your hearing and in your speaking, in your thinking
and in your doing. Listen for the word of God.

Response to the Word (Colossians 3)
What would our lives look like
if we did everything in the name of Jesus?
    We would reflect the face of God.
What would our words sound like
if everything we spoke was in the name of Jesus?
    We would echo the voice of Christ.

What would our world be like
if everything gave praise and glory to God
with gratitude and joy?
Heaven would come to earth.

Thanksgiving and Communion

Invitation to the Offering (1 Samuel 2, Colossians 3)

As Hannah gave her firstborn son, Samuel, to God, so now we offer our lives and our gifts to God. God does not demand such sacrifice, and yet our gifts are pleasing to God. With gratitude and love, we offer our gifts, that God's love may clothe the world.

Offering Prayer (Colossians 3)

Generous God, clothe these gifts with love and kindness,
that all who receive our ministry and our gifts:
may know your love and mercy,
may touch the peace of Christ,
and may live in communion
with the Holy Spirit. Amen.

Sending Forth

Benediction (Colossians 3)

May the word of Christ live in you richly.
May the love of God clothe you with compassion
and kindness.
May the power of the Holy Spirit grant you peace,
both now and forever more.

Contributors

Laura Jaquith Bartlett, an ordained minister of music and worship, lives at a United Methodist adult retreat center in the foothills of Oregon's Mount Hood, where she serves as the program director, as well as doing worship consulting and coaching.

B. J. Beu is senior pastor of Neighborhood Congregational Church in Laguna Beach, California. A graduate of Boston University and Pacific Lutheran University, Beu loves creative worship, preaching, and advocating for peace and justice. Find out more at B. J.'s church website www.ncclaguna.org

Mary Petrina Boyd is pastor of Langley United Methodist Church on Whidbey Island. She spends alternating summers working as an archaeologist in Jordan.

Joanne Carlson Brown is the clergy-type for Tibbetts United Methodist Church in Seattle, Washington. She is also an adjunct professor at Seattle University School of Theology and Ministry and lives in Seattle with Thistle, the wee Westie.

Karen Ellis is a United Methodist pastor who lives in Tustin, California with her husband and two children.

Safiyah Fosua serves as assistant professor of Christian Ministry and Congregational Worship at Wesley Seminary at Indiana Wesleyan University and is a clergy member of the Greater New Jersey Annual Conference.

Rebecca J. Kruger Gaudino, a United Church of Christ minister in Portland, Oregon, teaches world religions and biblical studies as visiting professor at the University of Portland and also writes for the Church.

Jamie Greening is a Southern Baptist pastor and writer who blogs at www.jdgreening.wordpress.com.

Bill Hoppe is the music coordinator for Bear Creek United Methodist Church in Woodinville, Washington, and is a member of the band BrokenWorks, for which he is the keyboardist. He thanks his family and friends for their continued love, support, and inspiration.

Amy B. Hunter is a poet, spiritual director, and Episcopal layperson. Her work tends to be Christian formation, but her passion is answering God's call to her to write. Two outcomes of her writing life are *A Table in the Wilderness*, available at Lulu.com, and a blog, Astrolabe and Trope (http://astrolabeandtrope.wordpress.com/).

Carol Cook Moore is an elder in the United Methodist Church and assistant professor of Worship and Preaching at Wesley Theological Seminary, Washington, D.C.

J. Wayne Pratt is a retired local pastor living in Wake Forest, North Carolina. A graduate of Drew Theological

School, Wayne is the author of *Sanctuary: Prayers from the Garden, Just in Time! Wedding Services*, and *Worship in the Garden: Services for Outdoor Worship*. He enjoys preaching, writing, and gardening.

Mary J. Scifres serves as a consultant in church leadership, worship, and evangelism from her Laguna Beach home, where she and her spouse, B. J., reside with their teenage son, Michael. Her books include *The United Methodist Music and Worship Planner, Just in Time! Special Services, Prepare!* and *Searching for Seekers*. Find out more at Mary's website, www.maryscifres.com

Deborah Sokolove is associate professor of Art and Worship at Wesley Theological Seminary, where she also serves as the director of the Henry Luce III Center for the Arts and Religion.

Indexes

Page numbers in italics refer to the online-only material.

Scripture Index

Communion Liturgy Index

Liturgies in italics are online-only material.

For download access to the online material, click on the link for *The Abingdon Worship Annual 2015* at abingdonpress.com/downloads, and when prompted, enter the password: worship2015.